INTRODUCTION TO THE RODIN COLLECTION

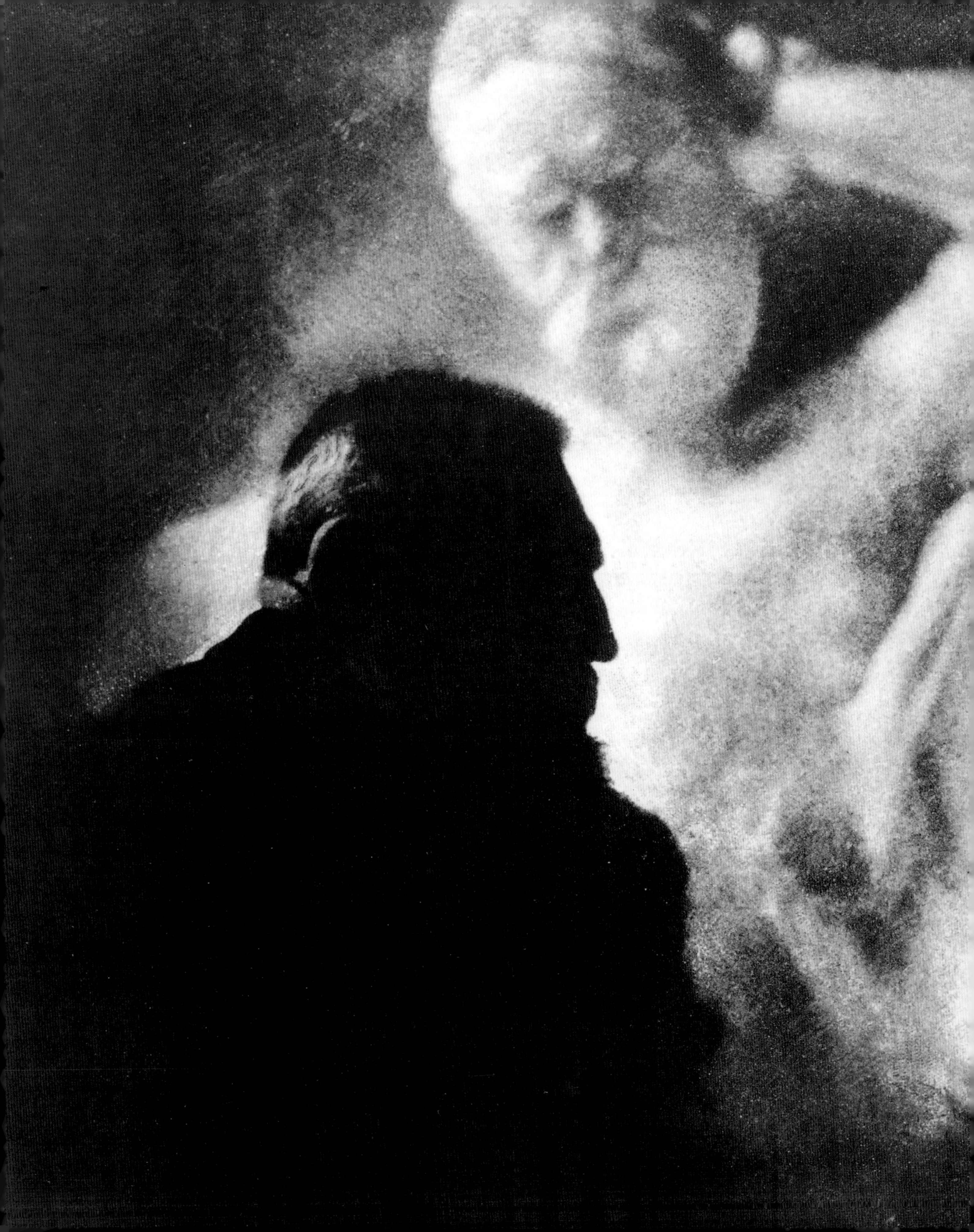

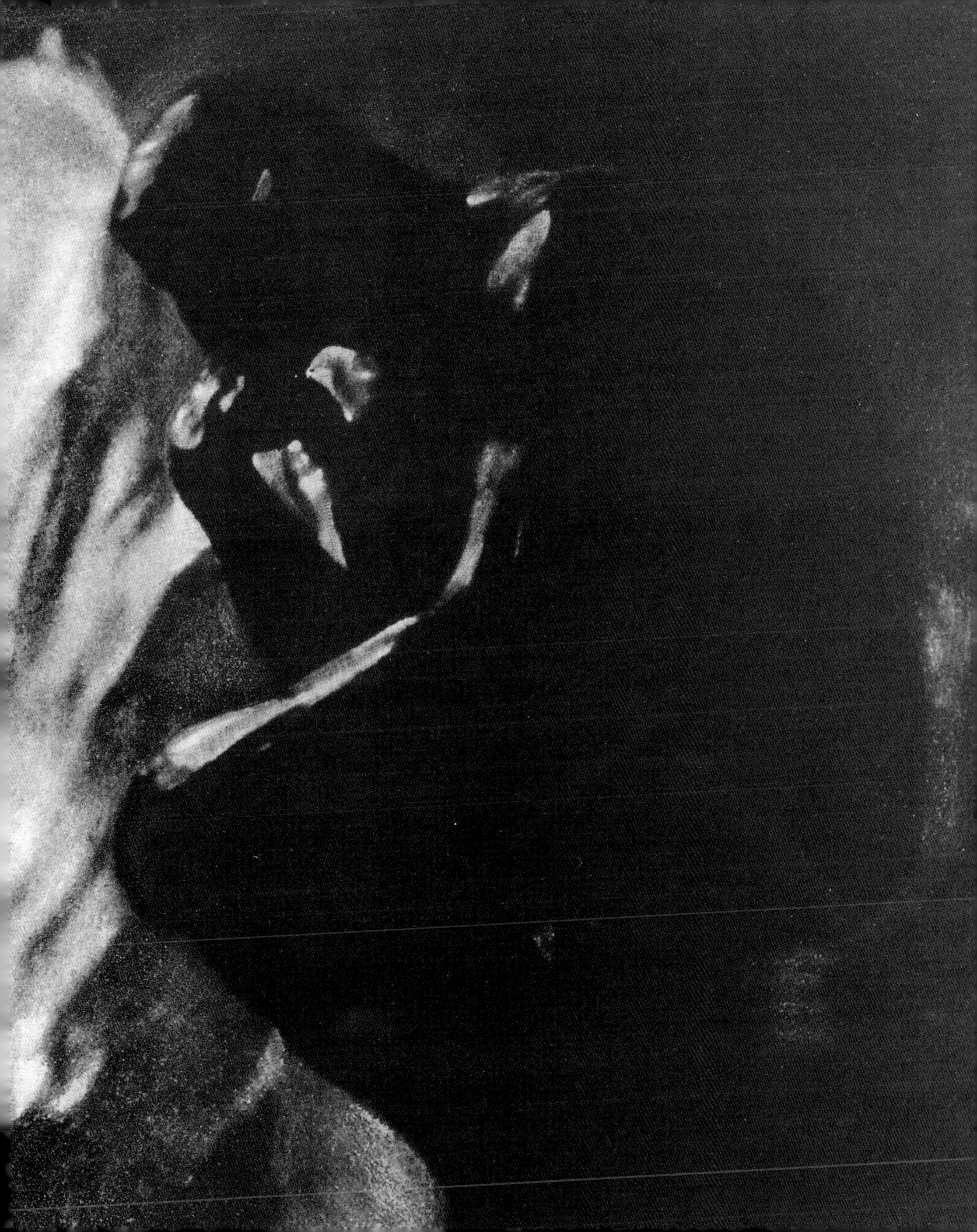

Ro

INTRODUCTION TO THE RODIN COLLECTION

of the Iris & B. Gerald Cantor Center for Visual Arts at Stanford University

including the B. Gerald Cantor Rodin Sculpture Garden

ALBERT ELSEN

Edited and revised by Bernard Barryte

din

Unless otherwise specified, the works illustrated are gifts of Iris and B. Gerald Cantor or the Iris and B. Gerald Cantor Foundation, are by Auguste Rodin, and are in bronze. Dimensions are given in centimeters in the following order: height, width, depth. "Cat." references are to Albert E. Elsen with Rosalyn Frankel Jamison, Rodin's Art: The Rodin Collection of the Iris & B. Gerald Cantor Center for Visual Arts at Stanford University, *ed. Bernard Barryte (New York: Oxford University Press, 2003). The sculpture collection includes 197 works, only a portion of which are on view at any given time.*

Photography: Frank Wing, except the following: fig. 6, Bill Schaefer; fig. 10, Musée Rodin, Paris; fig. 14, Ecole Nationale Supérieure des Beaux-Arts; fig. 27, Philadelphia Museum of Art: Marion Angell Boyer and Francis Boyer Library; fig. 39, Becky Cohen; fig. 44, Bildarchiv Foto Marburg; fig. 58, Lee Fatherree; fig. 67, Bibliothèque Nationale, Paris; fig. 68, Photo Harlingue-Viollet, Paris

Library of Congress Cataloging-in-Publication Data
Iris & B. Gerald Cantor Center for Visual Arts at Stanford University
Introduction to the Rodin Collection of the Iris & B. Gerald Cantor Center for Visual Arts at Stanford University including the B. Gerald Cantor Rodin Sculpture Garden / Albert Elsen; edited and revised by Bernard Barryte
p. cm
Includes bibliographical references.
ISBN 0-937031-22-4 (alk. paper)
1. Rodin, Auguste, 1840–1917—Catalogs. 2. Bronze sculpture—California—Palo Alto—Catalogs. 3. Iris & B. Gerald Cantor Center for Visual Arts at Stanford University—Catalogs. I. Elsen, Albert Edward, 1927–1995. II. Barryte, Bernard. III. Title.
NB553.R7A4 2003A
730'.92—dc22 200305667

COVER Etienne Carjet (1829–1906), *Portrait of Auguste Rodin*, c. 1885, woodburytype, 21.8 × 16.3, Gift of Albert E. Elsen, 1994.55 (cat. A72)

FRONTISPIECE Edward Steichen (1879–1973), *Rodin—Le Penseur* (detail), 1902, offset lithograph, printed in *Camera Work*, July 1905, 16.5 × 18.4, 1988.263 (cat. A87)

Publication of *Introduction to the Rodin Collection* is made possible by generous support from an anonymous donor.

CONTENTS

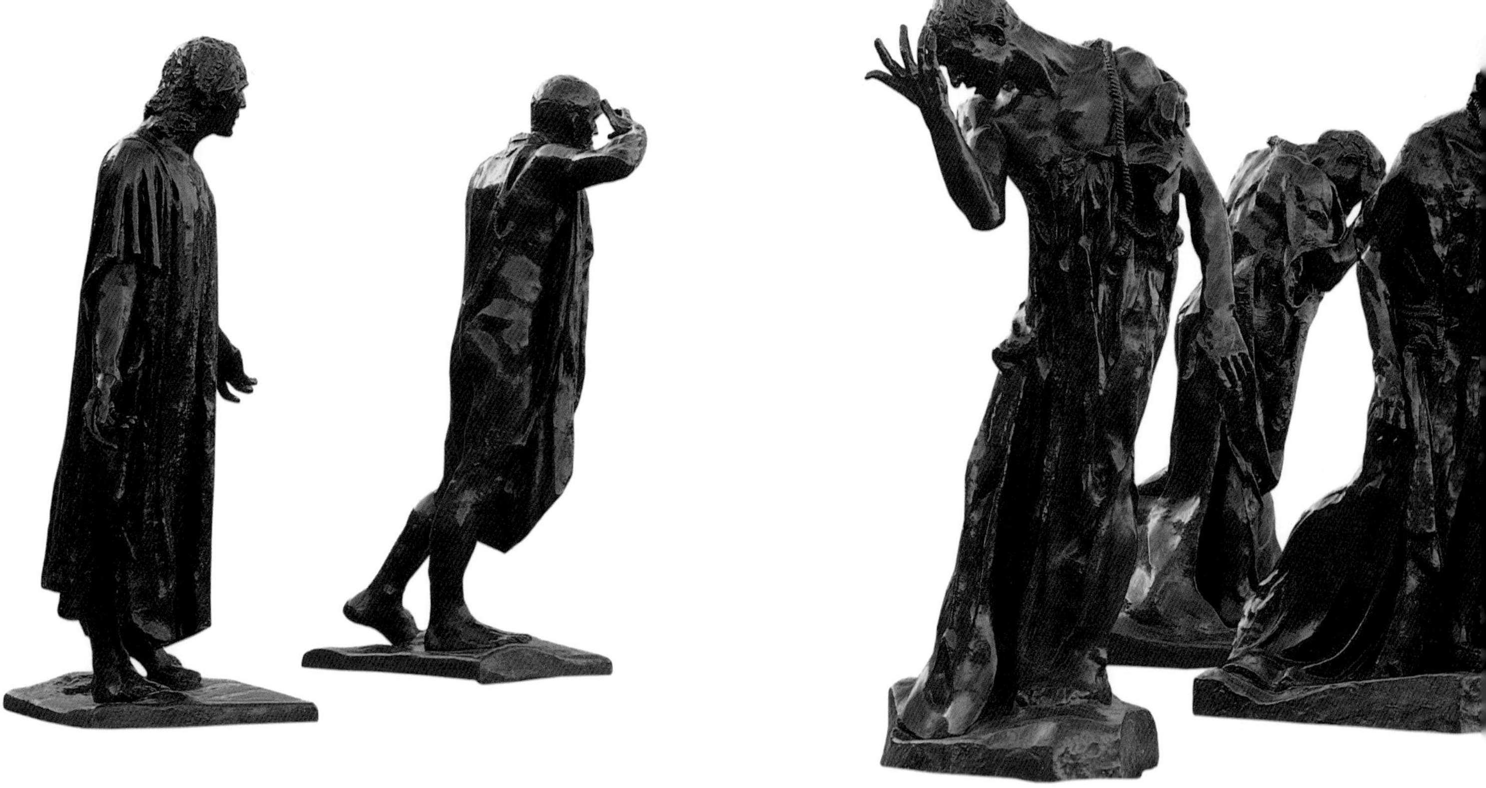

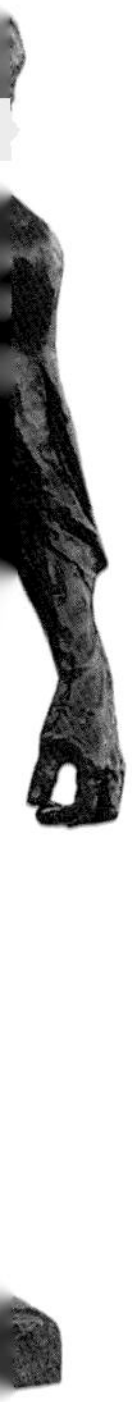

FOREWORD

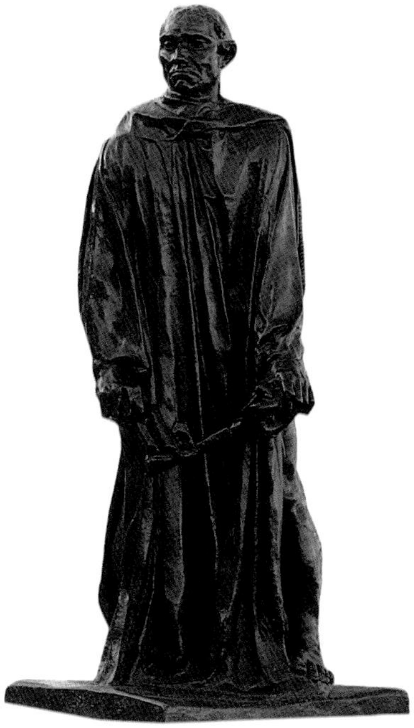

As a result of the generosity of Iris and B. Gerald Cantor, Stanford University possesses one of the largest collections of Rodin's sculpture in the world and the only collection developed explicitly to illustrate the breadth of the artist's accomplishment. It was the donors' wish that the collection be used for study and pleasure by scholars, the academic community, and the public. Consequently *The Burghers of Calais* is on view in Memorial Court, and twenty-one large-scale works are illuminated at night and accessible twenty-four hours a day in the B. Gerald Cantor Rodin Sculpture Garden.[1] In addition, a selection of smaller works are on view in the Cantor Arts Center during regular museum hours. Works in storage may be seen by appointment. These include sculptures, prints, and drawings by Rodin as well as historic documentary photographs of the sculptor and his creations.

This booklet is intended as an introduction to the sculptor and the collection of his work at Stanford University. It is based upon two brochures, *The B. G. Cantor Collection Rodin Journal* (1982) and *The B. Gerald Cantor Rodin Sculpture Garden* (1987), written by Professor Albert Elsen (1927–1995), who worked with Mr. Cantor to develop Stanford's collection. These texts have been revised and augmented by Chief Curator Bernard Barryte to include information from other sources, in particular Elsen's catalogue of the collection, *Rodin's Art* (2003), which discusses the individual works in detail. We are grateful to the anonymous donor whose generosity has made this publication possible.

THOMAS K. SELIGMAN *Jill & John Freidenrich Director*

1. This one-acre site was dedicated in May 1985 to honor the donor of most of Stanford's Rodin collection. Paid for by private donations and by the university, the garden was originally designed by architect Robert Mittelstadt. His design was modified by landscape architect John Wong of the SWA Group as part of the reconstruction preceding the reopening of the museum in 1999, a decade after the Loma Prieta earthquake had forced it to close. On the original design, see Robert Mittelstadt and Albert E. Elsen, "The B. Gerald Cantor Rodin Sculpture Garden at Stanford University," *International Journal of Museum Management and Curatorship* 7 (1988): 173–84.

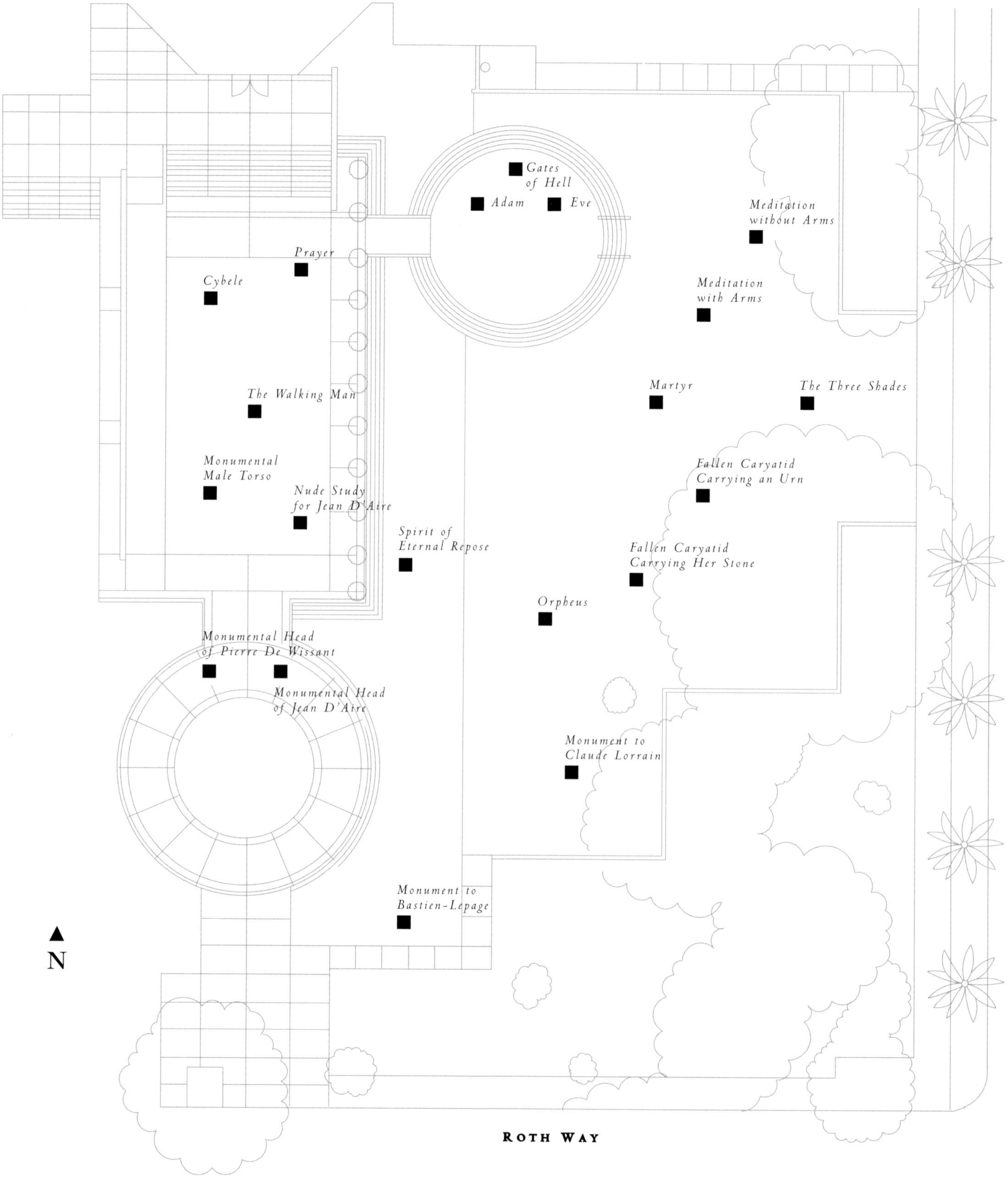

B. Gerald Cantor Rodin Sculpture Garden, Stanford University

INTRODUCTION TO THE RODIN COLLECTION

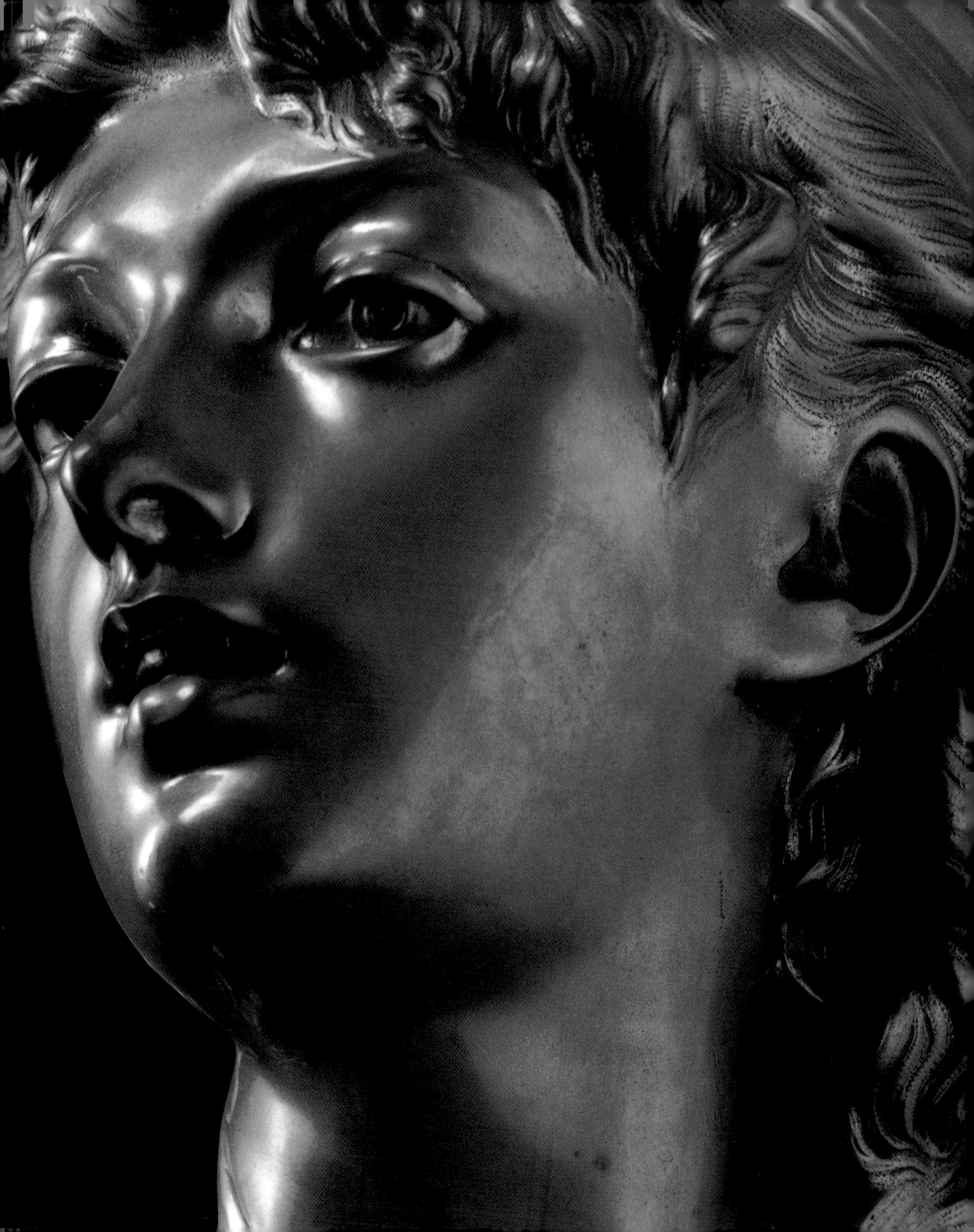

Rodin

A CAREER IN SCULPTURE

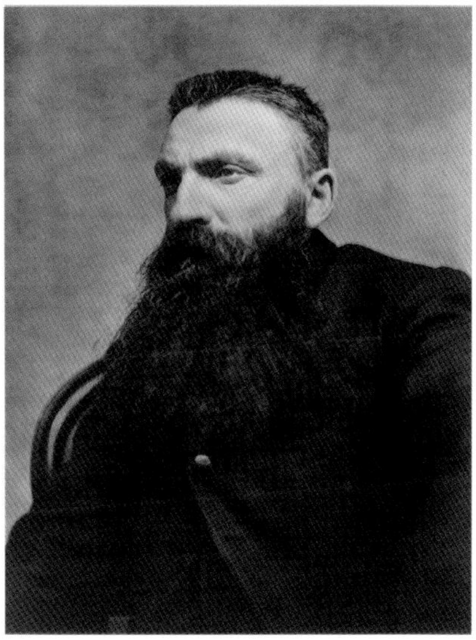

[OPPOSITE]
Suzon (detail), 1875
Cie des Bronzes foundry, c. 1900
43.8 × 21.9 × 21.9
1975.15 (cat. 129)

1
[ABOVE]
Etienne Carjet (1829–1906)
Portrait of Auguste Rodin, c. 1885
Woodburytype
21.8 × 16.3
Gift of Albert E. Elsen, 1994.55 (cat. A72)

François-Auguste-René Rodin (1840–1917; fig. 1) made his public debut as a maker of statues in 1877, when his life was almost half over.[1] Born into a lower-middle-class family in Paris, Rodin had little formal education, prompting one eminent art historian to mistakenly categorize him as "ignorant." His training as a professional artist was limited to attendance at the Ecole des Dessins from 1854 to 1857, during which time he distinguished himself in drawing under the tutelage of Horace Lecoq de Boisbaudran (1802–1897) and also discovered modeling. The young artist thrice failed the entrance examination for the Ecole des Beaux-Arts, the prestigious government-sponsored school for training artists, primarily because his eighteenth-century modeling style was unfashionable and did not find favor with the entrance committee.

As a result, Rodin was largely self-educated as a sculptor, but that education was enriched by contact with the sculptors who employed him and with fellow decorative artists. In addition, he frequented the Louvre and other museums as well as the annual Salons. Displaying hundreds of sculptures and paintings, these vast public exhibitions were especially important for young artists. In the eyes of most potential patrons and of the public generally, acceptance by the Salon jury—composed of artists, academicians, and important officials—constituted a form of professional accreditation. Moreover, careers were advanced or retarded by the innumerable French and foreign critics who reviewed these immensely popular events. Thus Rodin formed his own style from direct exposure to the classical and medieval traditions and, most importantly, from works by his older contemporaries, sculptors of the Second Empire and early Third Republic such as the famous sculptor of animals Antoine-Louis Barye (1796–1875) and the versatile Jean-Baptiste Carpeaux (1827–1875).

Resigned to supporting himself as a decorative sculptor, Rodin worked primarily for other artists between 1857 and 1882. They signed their names to his work, as was then customary and as Rodin would in turn do with the work of his own assistants. (From the mid-1870s he managed to employ at least one assistant to help him on his own creations.) The upheavals of the Franco-Prussian War and the Commune (1870–71) diminished opportunities for employment in Paris, so that Rodin was obliged to support himself, his mistress Rose Beuret, and their son by working in Belgium from 1871 until 1877. Earnings from journeyman work such as carving figures for the Bourse at Brussels and from the sale of commercially appealing figures such as *Suzon* (fig. 2)[2] also helped finance a trip to Italy in 1875. Seeing the marbles and bronzes of Michelangelo, Donatello, and others was crucial to Rodin's development and affirmed his determination to be a maker of statues.

Rodin first achieved notoriety at the Salon of 1877 with *The Age of Bronze* (fig. 3). This statue provoked a furious controversy among critics, who debated whether the lifelike figure had in fact been modeled by the sculptor or whether Rodin had merely made a cast from a man's living body. In the end the sculptor was vindicated and his virtuosity acknowledged. Moreover, the notoriety proved beneficial, resulting in commissions that launched the thirty-seven-year-old sculptor's career and enabled him to return permanently to Paris.

Even before he left for Belgium, however, Rodin's hands had been famous among his fellow workers for their speed and dexterity in fashioning works in a variety of styles. Later in life he would complain of bad habits acquired from the type of work circumstances had obliged him to produce—ornament designs, architectural reliefs, objets d'art, and ceramic decoration in the factory at Sèvres (fig. 4)—but such work also contributed to his lifelong love of *métier*, or craft. His signature style of working directly from the model was formed early with the *Mask of the Man with the Broken Nose* (fig. 5). Although it had been rejected by the Salon jury in 1864, Rodin later told the American sculptor Truman H. Bartlett that he considered this portrait of a laborer named Bibi to be "the first good piece of modeling I ever did." He further explained that it served as a paradigm for all his subsequent

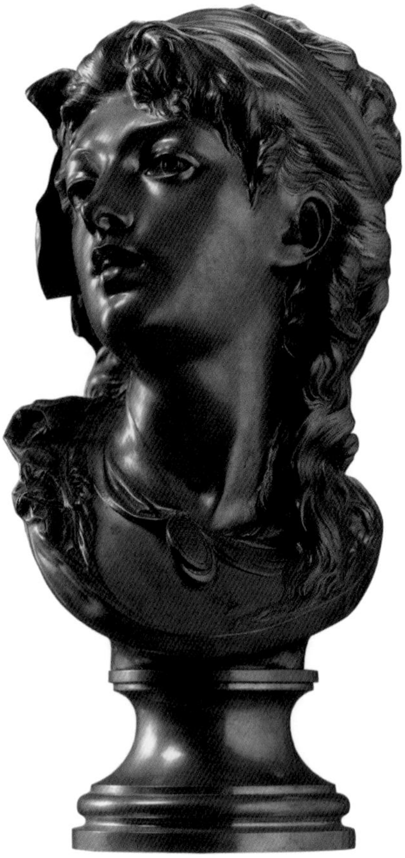

2
[ABOVE]
Suzon, 1875
Cie des Bronzes
foundry, c. 1900
43.8 × 21.9 × 21.9
1975.15 (cat. 129)

3
[OPPOSITE]
The Age of Bronze, 1875–76,
reduced 1903–4
Plaster, Alexis Rudier foundry
65 × 21.6 × 17.8
1984.431 (cat. 3)

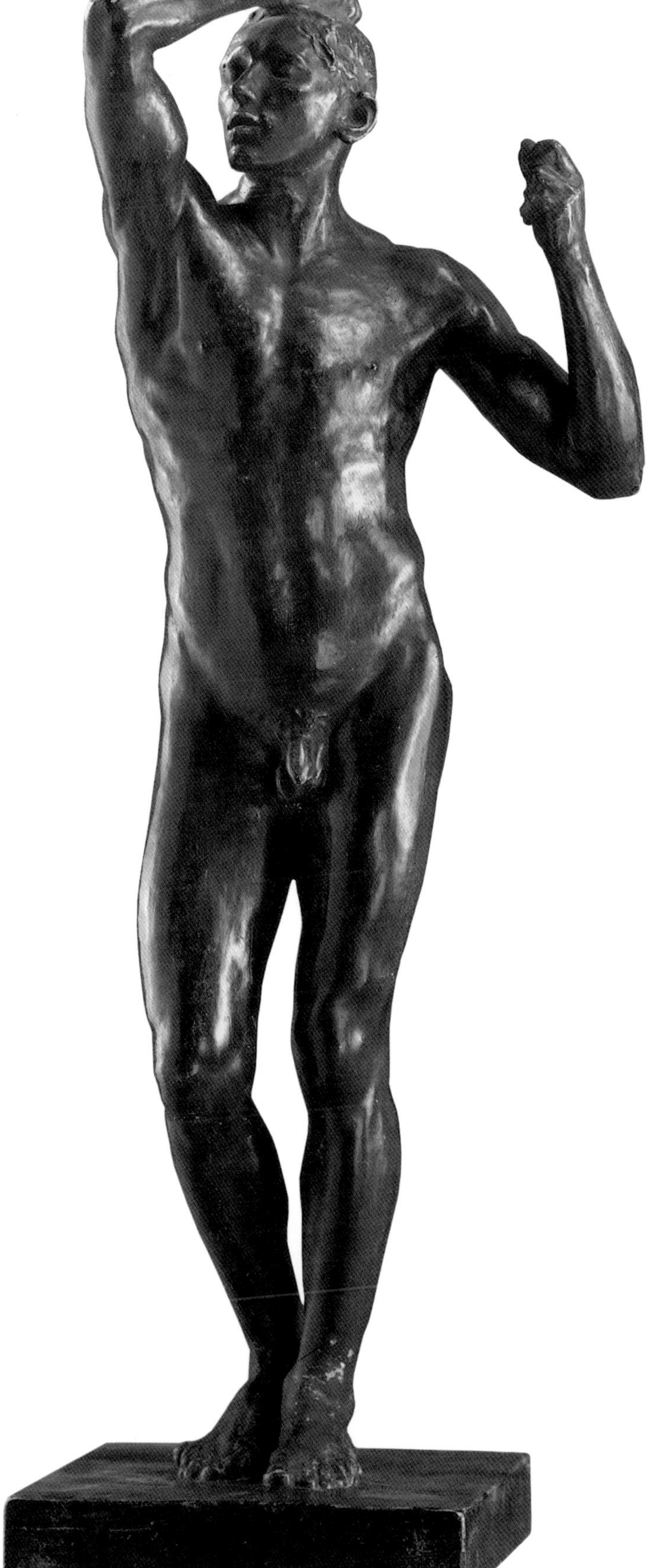

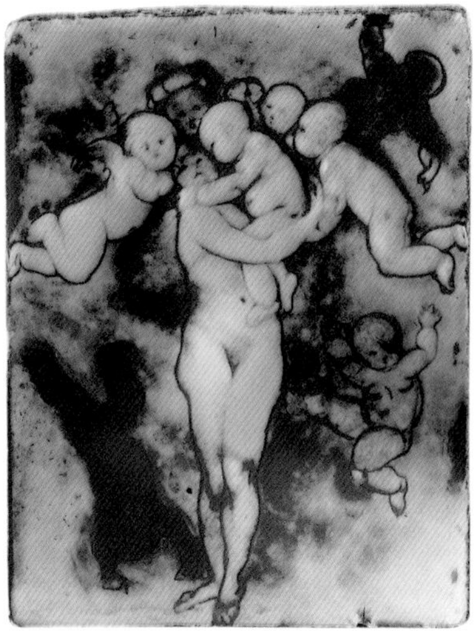

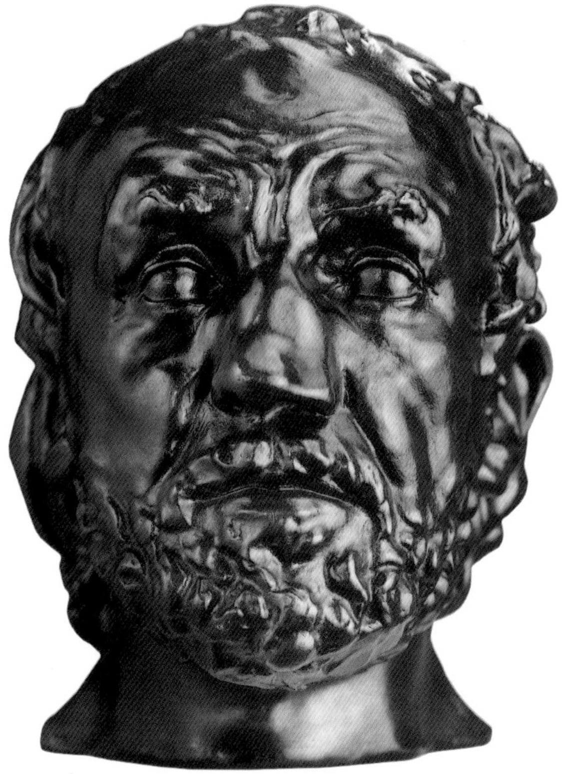

4
[ABOVE LEFT]
Springtime, c. 1880–82
Glazed porcelain
10.5 × 8
Gift of Mme Lascelle de Basily,
1974.192.2 (cat. 196)

5
[ABOVE RIGHT]
Mask of the Man with the Broken Nose, 1863–64
Posthumous cast
27.9 × 20.3 × 21.6
1974.74 (cat. 125)

6
[OPPOSITE]
The Gates of Hell
with *Adam* and *Eve*

work because in it were distilled the two abiding principles of his art: the direct apprehension of nature and the vivid realization of complex form in three dimensions.[3]

Contrary to the popular notion that Rodin was ignored or rejected by the French government, many of his works were purchased by the Ministry of Fine Arts, and by the late 1870s he had begun to make lifelong friends among influential politicians, who furthered his career. Three years after he exhibited *The Age of Bronze*, Rodin received the first of several major state commissions, *The Gates of Hell*, which occupied him on and off over the next two decades (fig. 6). During this period he produced other monumental public sculptures such as *The Burghers of Calais* (fig. 58) and the monuments to the painter Claude Lorrain (fig. 7) and the writer Honoré de Balzac (1891). Rodin began to submit work to international exhibitions in the 1870s. A decade later his stature was acknowledged by the receipt of invitations to participate in exhibitions throughout Europe. His fame, however, as well as his financial independence, was initially derived from portraits such

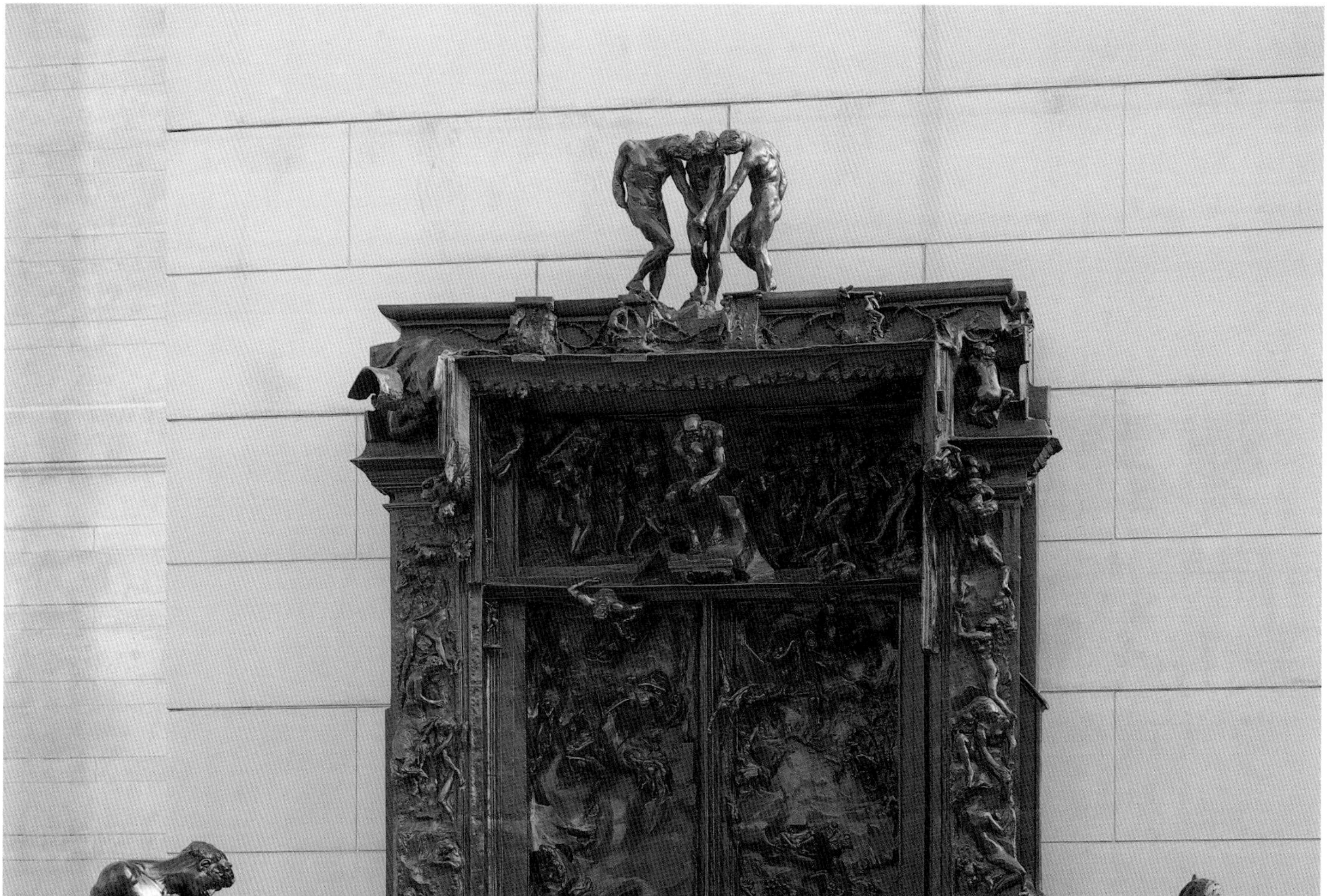

as *Bust of Madame Morla Vicuña* (fig. 8), made in the 1880s. Thereafter, his most venturesome work was done on a small scale, and after 1894 many of his earlier small sculptures were enlarged by his "perfect collaborator," the excellent technician Henri Lebossé (1845–1922), who specialized in such work. Although Rodin's sculptures remained controversial, reviews and notices by critics and journalists were increasingly favorable from the 1880s onward, and he powerfully influenced the younger generation of artists. By the time of the great retrospective Rodin produced for himself in 1900, he was frequently lauded in newspapers and journals, and his international clientele included aristocrats, politicians, and millionaires. When he died in 1917, Rodin was probably the most famous artist in the world.

A man of prodigious creative energy, Rodin could not have sustained his reputation without the assistance of the professional craftsmen who carved his marbles, enlarged or reduced his figures, and cast his bronzes. Such collaboration between sculptor and craftsmen or foundrymen was both conventional and economically necessary in the competitive, commercialized art world of nineteenth-century France, and his patrons were certainly well aware if it. Although Rodin accepted more commissions than even he could finish, his legendary inventiveness and numerous assistants did enable him to be exceptionally productive. He determined by 1900 to leave a museum of his art, and shortly before his death he gave all his property to the state, which established the first museum in France dedicated to a single artist. Rodin's bequest included his collection of classical and Asian art, works by his contemporaries (many acquired as gifts), and a vast archive of photographs and correspondence. Most importantly it included more than seven thousand of his own drawings and the staggering collection of about eight thousand models, fragments, and completed works in various media that is divided between the two former residences that today constitute the Musée Rodin in Paris and its reserve at Meudon.[4]

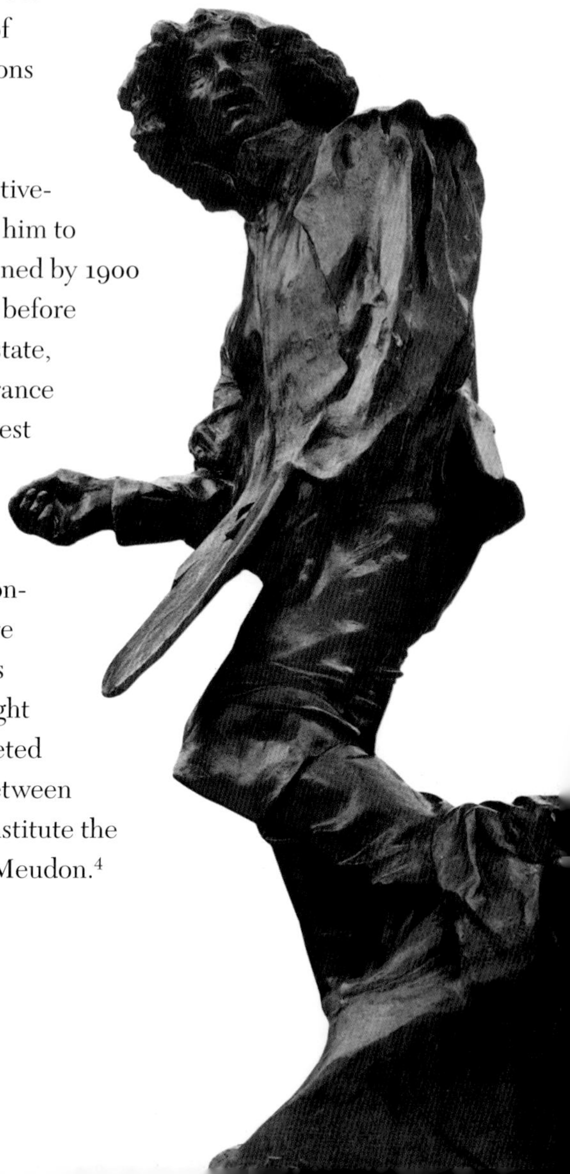

7
Claude Lorrain, Final Version, 1889
Cast 1983, 1/8
214.6 × 108 × 116.8
1992.154 (cat. 95)

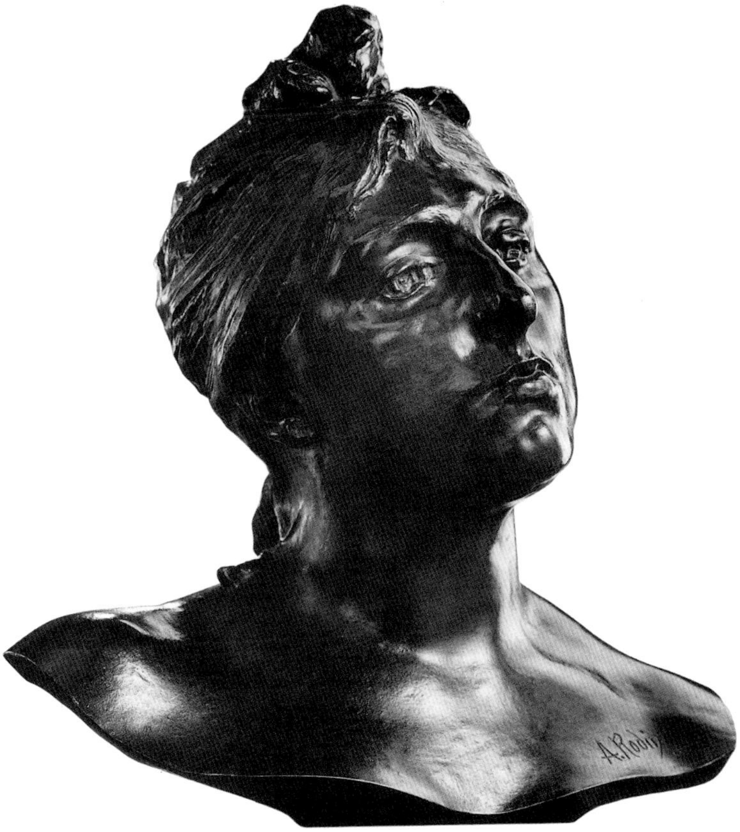

8
[LEFT]
Bust of Madame Morla Vicuña, 1884
Cast 1972, 1/12
39 × 36 × 26.7
1974.68 (cat. 133)

9
[BELOW]
Cast of Rodin's Hand with a Small Torso, 1917
Cast 1973, 8/12
17.8 × 22.9 × 39.4
1974.48 (cat. 194)

In addition, Rodin willed the state his copyright. This gave it the right to authorize the production of posthumous casts—since 1946, limited by the museum to twelve and, since 1981, limited by French law to eight casts for the art market and four for cultural institutions—such as those included in Stanford's collection.[5]

Rodin: The Man

From contemporary photographs and descriptions we are well acquainted with Rodin's appearance. In 1887 Truman Bartlett described him as about five feet seven inches tall, weighing 140 pounds, with strong, "beautiful hands," as can be seen in *Cast of Rodin's Hand with a Small Torso* (fig. 9), a composition that includes a cast of the sculptor's hand made by Paul Cruet

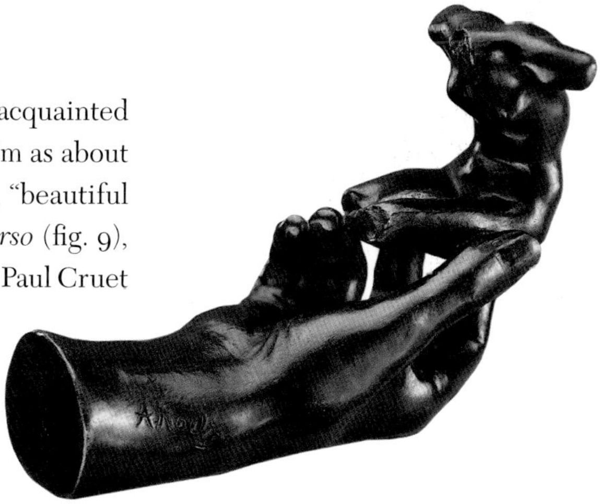

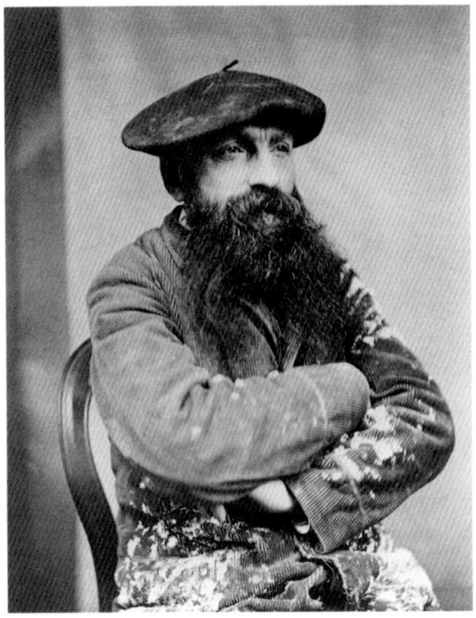

10
Photographer unknown
Rodin with Arms Crossed, 1880
Albumen print
21.8 × 16.8
Collection Musée Rodin, Paris
See page 68 for larger version of this image

about three weeks prior to Rodin's death.[6] The critic Gustave Geffroy introduced the sculptor to his readers with a particularly vivid characterization:

> The man who stands before you, his hands covered with wet clay, his clothes splashed with plaster is short and sturdy as to figure, peculiarly tranquil as to manner. He has no specially salient features, yet his physiognomy as a whole is full of character. Framed by the close-cut hair and the long fair beard . . . we see a mobile face. . . . The brow . . . is that of a thinker. The gently aquiline nose completes a profile that recalls the profiles of sculptured monks in cathedral porches. But this is a monk full of human sympathies and subtleties, armed with critical faculty and force of will, and haunted . . . by modern questionings and also by modern solutions.[7]

The sculptor had about him the air of the worker, and though ennobled by his "Olympian" beard, until about 1900 he was frequently seen with clay and plaster on his clothes (fig. 10). Many were impressed by his aura of tranquility or, as Bartlett put it, "his philosophical healthiness," although Bartlett also observed that Rodin was "tormented by a turbulent imagination."[8]

Contemporary sources generally agree that the soft-spoken sculptor was without guile, and many commented on his lack of pretension, his resoluteness, and his tenacity. By nature he was a private person. The critic Camille Mauclair characterized him as "courteous, precise, and reserved," noting that "little by little the initial impression of timidity becomes one of authority."[9] Unlike Honoré de Balzac (1799–1850), the renowned author who was the subject of one of Rodin's most controversial monuments, the sculptor lived to work well, rather than the reverse, and he had no ambition to be other than he was, perhaps because of his abiding confidence in his own vision and its worth. Rodin regarded people as though sizing them up for a sculpture, as Bartlett noted: "He judges people as absolutely as he does art: on principle, mercilessly; on the score of sympathy, with the tenderness of a warm and considerate heart."[10] Many newspaper reporters referred to the "genial Rodin," lauding his kindliness and accessibility, and it is doubtful that he ever refused an interview or that a visitor to the studio went away disappointed. He was a natural teacher, and his discourse on his own art touched others with its conviction and decisiveness. "Standing before a statue," Mauclair observed, "Rodin has a very curious way of making you understand his intentions; it is at once elliptical and perfectly clear."[11] Always grateful for kindness, favors, and favorable reviews, the sculptor wrote terse but appreciative notes by the hundreds to express his gratitude. When honors came, he seems to have worn them lightly. Although he sometimes alienated admirers, Rodin also sustained friendships over long periods of time, and he used his prestige to help countless other artists.

Rodin was unsophisticated but wise. He knew depression but never paralyzing self-doubt, although he endured more than his fair share of injustice and half a lifetime of hardship. He responded to reverses and misfortunes with patience and persistence but never forgot defeats, and late in life these seemed almost more important than his victories. Vindication rather than vengeance was his goal. He habitually shared reminiscences of his modest upbringing and life of serious labor. Work, not theology, was Rodin's path to salvation.

The sculptor was attractive to men and to women. He did not discourage a reputation as a womanizer, and yet he was capable of long-term friendships with women as well as affairs. Rodin seems to have been sexually active into old age—in 1906 one female sitter complained of being exhausted "by the need to fight for my dignity against his hunter's gaze."[12] He was a poor parent, however, withholding not only his name but also his affection from his son after a childhood accident left the boy with brain damage.

While Rodin may have fitted the public's stereotype of the artist in his appearance and manner, in other respects he did not. In particular, he was extremely well organized and businesslike, maintaining careful records of business transactions and correspondence, and mastering the politicized system of the arts in the Third Republic to secure prestigious commissions, fame, and financial well-being. Although fiercely patriotic, he avoided national politics. Evidence indicates that he was a Republican, for he entered patriotic competitions after 1871 and modeled portraits of such prominent Republicans as the writer Victor Hugo, the radical journalist Henri Rochefort, and the politician Georges Clemenceau (fig. 11). Nevertheless, although Emile Zola had secured for Rodin the commission for the monument to Balzac, the sculptor stayed out of the Dreyfus Affair, to which Zola was deeply committed (a possible reason being Rodin's disinclination to add to his personal woes following the humiliating rejection of his bold and unprecedented composition). Rodin was against child labor laws because he saw them as the death knell for the ancient apprentice system by which young artists learned their craft.

Rather than rebelling against the prevailing art establishment, Rodin worked his way upward within it, gradually transforming taste through the power of his art. He always knew that strict academicians found his work technically unacceptable and considered the innovations he introduced

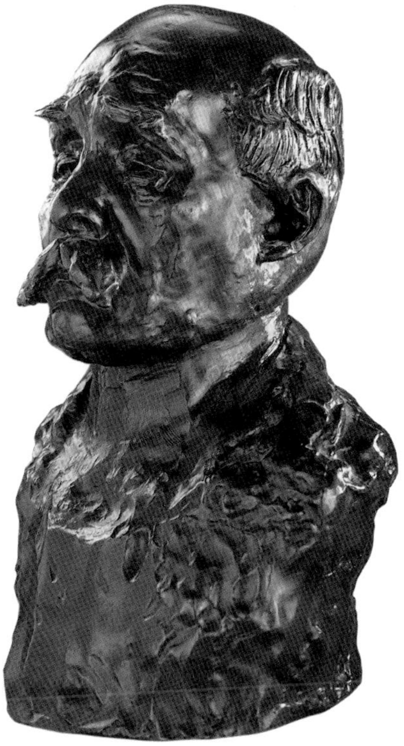

11
Bust of Georges Clemenceau, 1914
Cast 1970, 12/12
47.9 × 27.9 × 27.9
1974.67 (cat. 145)

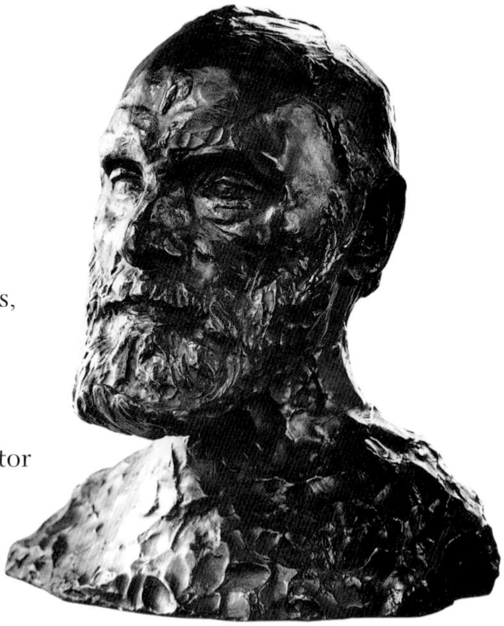

12
Bust of Eugène Guillaume, 1903
Cast 1972, 6/12
35.6 × 31.1 × 25.4
1974.73 (cat. 116)

offensive. Nevertheless, the sculptor made friends with other key figures in the art hierarchy—ministers of fine art, critics, and museum officials—often by inviting them to his studio, modeling their portraits, and thanking them for their kindness in letters and with gifts of his art. Late in life he even modeled a portrait of Eugène Guillaume (fig. 12), the conservative sculptor who, as the head of the Ecole des Beaux-Arts, had descried *The Age of Bronze* but who came to appreciate Rodin's accomplishments three decades later. Rodin learned to live with both notoriety and controversy, welcoming fame when it came and accepting honors from a sense of having earned them. Feeling that such acclaim granted him a right to express his thoughts, he did pontificate about art during the last decades of his life. As prelate of the Parisian sculpture world, he cared for the widows of former rivals, saw that crippled sculptors were given jobs as museum guards, and helped younger artists secure for their work more desirable locations in the Salons. Rodin was a worker-pope who created like a god and toiled like a slave.

Rodin's Qualities of Mind

Rodin was not inclined to theorize about art, and most of his pronouncements concerned the formal goals that informed his creations and the methods he refined in striving to attain them. A dedicated empiricist, he labored incessantly to discover things for himself. In particular, he relished the investigative process as he gradually resolved compositional problems, often exploring multiple solutions en route. "Happiness," he declared, "is found in oneself; work brings it."[13] Characteristically, the books that he habitually carried in his pocket were original works of literature, never commentaries; Aeschylus, Dante, Shakespeare, Victor Hugo, and Charles Baudelaire were favorite authors (fig. 13). Rodin's passionate reading was enriched by contact with many of France's influential literary figures.[14] Although he associated with intellectuals, he could not be construed as one himself. He no more relied upon received opinions about art and letters than he repeated academic formulas in figural construction or in the canon of works he admired. In fact, he contributed to the modern appreciation of world art, offering written praise for classical forms, Gothic architecture, Japanese art, and Indian sculpture.[15]

Rodin thought best while working with his hands in clay, modeling directly from nature or revising his own compositions. As was pointed out by the poet Rainer Maria Rilke, who was Rodin's secretary from 1904 to 1905, the sculptor's art was founded not upon a great idea, but upon the surfaces he created.[16] He was intensely focused, holding firmly a few fruitful convictions: one was the imperative of mastering his craft; another, the belief that the expressive potential of the living human form was inexhaustible. Rodin did not wait for inspiration but always worked knowing that ideas would come during the process of creation.

Along with an exceptional visual memory, the sculptor possessed a gift for analogizing. Because his imagination was almost exclusively figure-centered, this meant relating all things, nature as well as abstract ideas, to the human figure. Rodin's genius lay in opening his art to his processes of thought so that the compositions he created would grow and change as he did. For this reason nothing he made was finished or unalterable. Art was a continuum, and everything he had previously done was susceptible to addition or subtraction, complication or simplification. Implicit in his practice of evolving individual forms as well as compositions over time was an aptitude—almost a compulsion—for critiquing his own work as well as an eagerness to explore in newer works the ramifications of his older ideas.

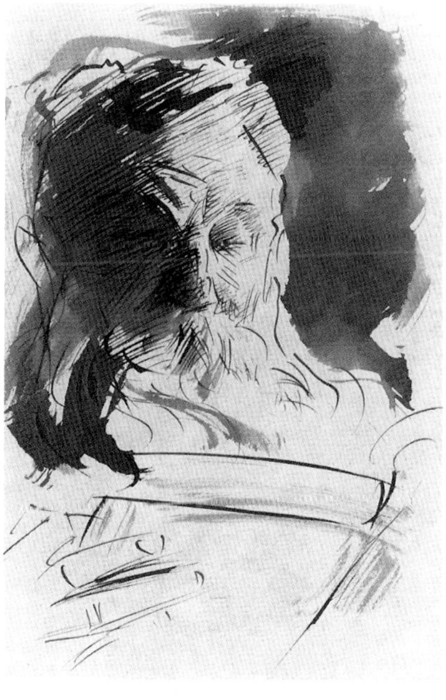

13
John Singer Sargent (1856–1925)
Portrait of Rodin Reading, 1902
Pen, ink, and wash on paper
18 × 11.8
1977.19 (cat. A52)

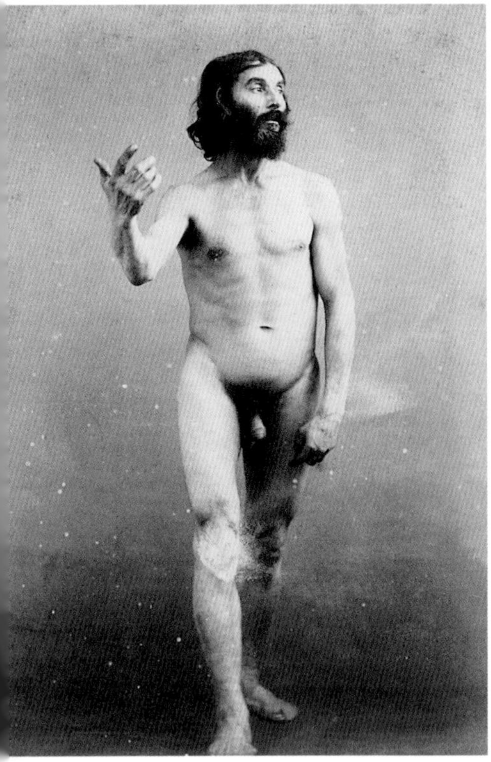

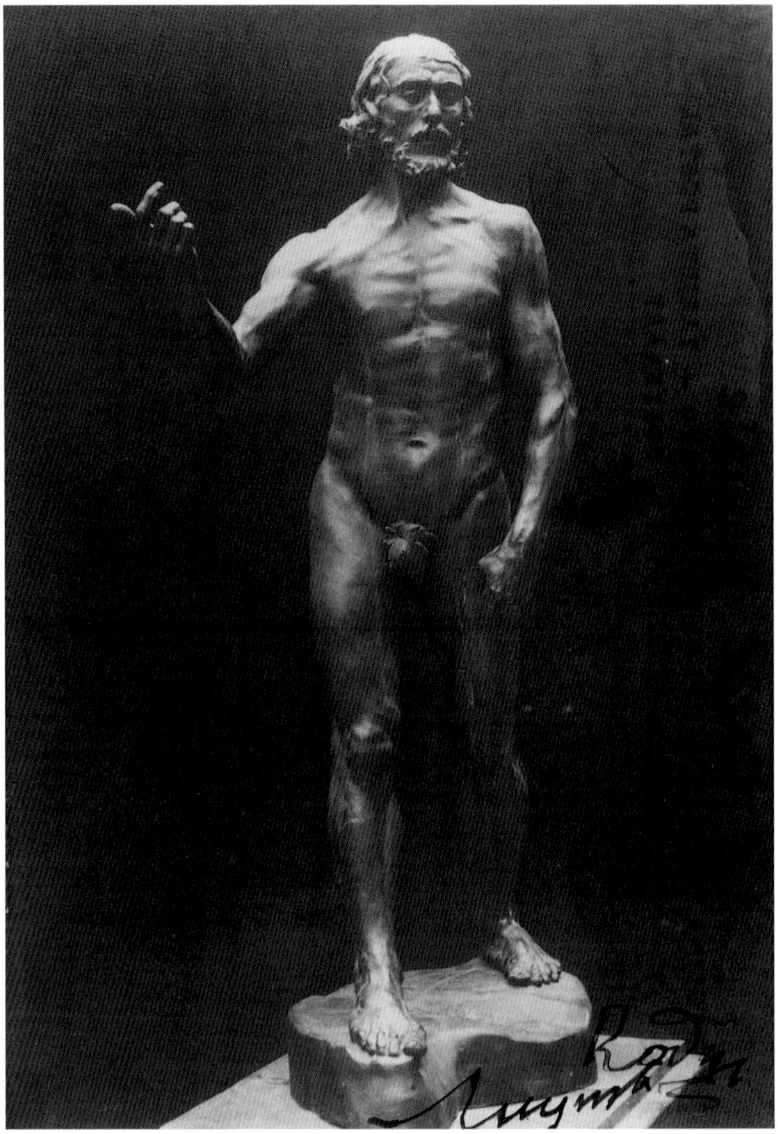

14
[ABOVE LEFT]
Photographer unknown
Pignatelli in the Pose of "Saint John the Baptist," after 1878
Gelatin silver print
Collection Ecole Nationale Supérieure des Beaux-Arts, Paris

15
[ABOVE RIGHT]
Etienne Neurdein (1832–c. 1910)
Postcard photograph of *Saint John the Baptist Preaching* in bronze
Albumen print
14 × 9
Museum general gifts, 1969.212.3 (cat. A157)

16
[OPPOSITE]
Torso of a Man, 1878
Cast 1979, 4/12
53.3 × 27.3 × 38.1
1983.200 (cat. 173)

Coupled with this was an inventive frugality which permitted him to get the most with the least, as when he invented dip-casting of plaster to obtain a new surface or when he created new compositions through surprising grafts and improbable but compelling unions from among the vast archive of figures and partial figures he maintained in his studio.[17] Rodin never let a good idea go to waste, even if it took years to rework it or if decades—and other applications or revisions—intervened between the initial modeling and subsequent reuse. For example, it is possible to trace the creation and reappearance of one favored torso over a thirty-year period. In 1878 the Italian Pignatelli served as the model for Rodin's *Saint John the Baptist Preaching* (figs. 14, 15). The torso (fig. 16), plaster casts of which had been made

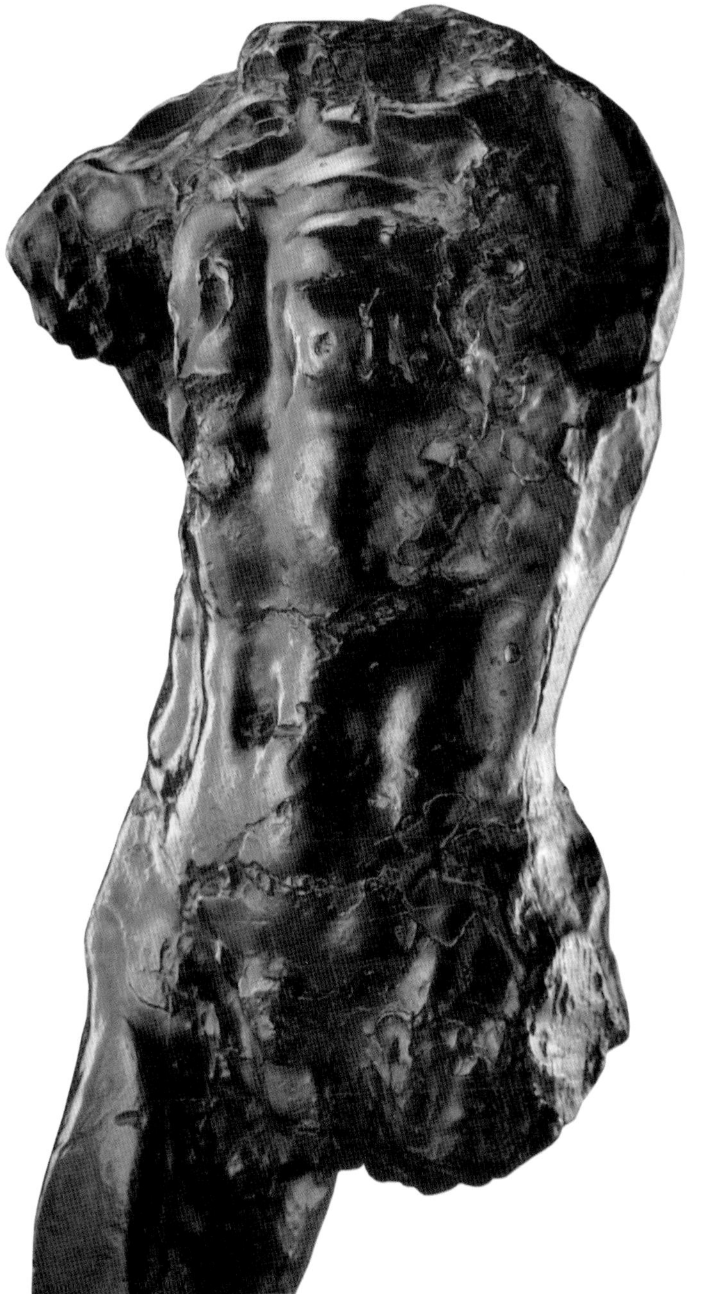

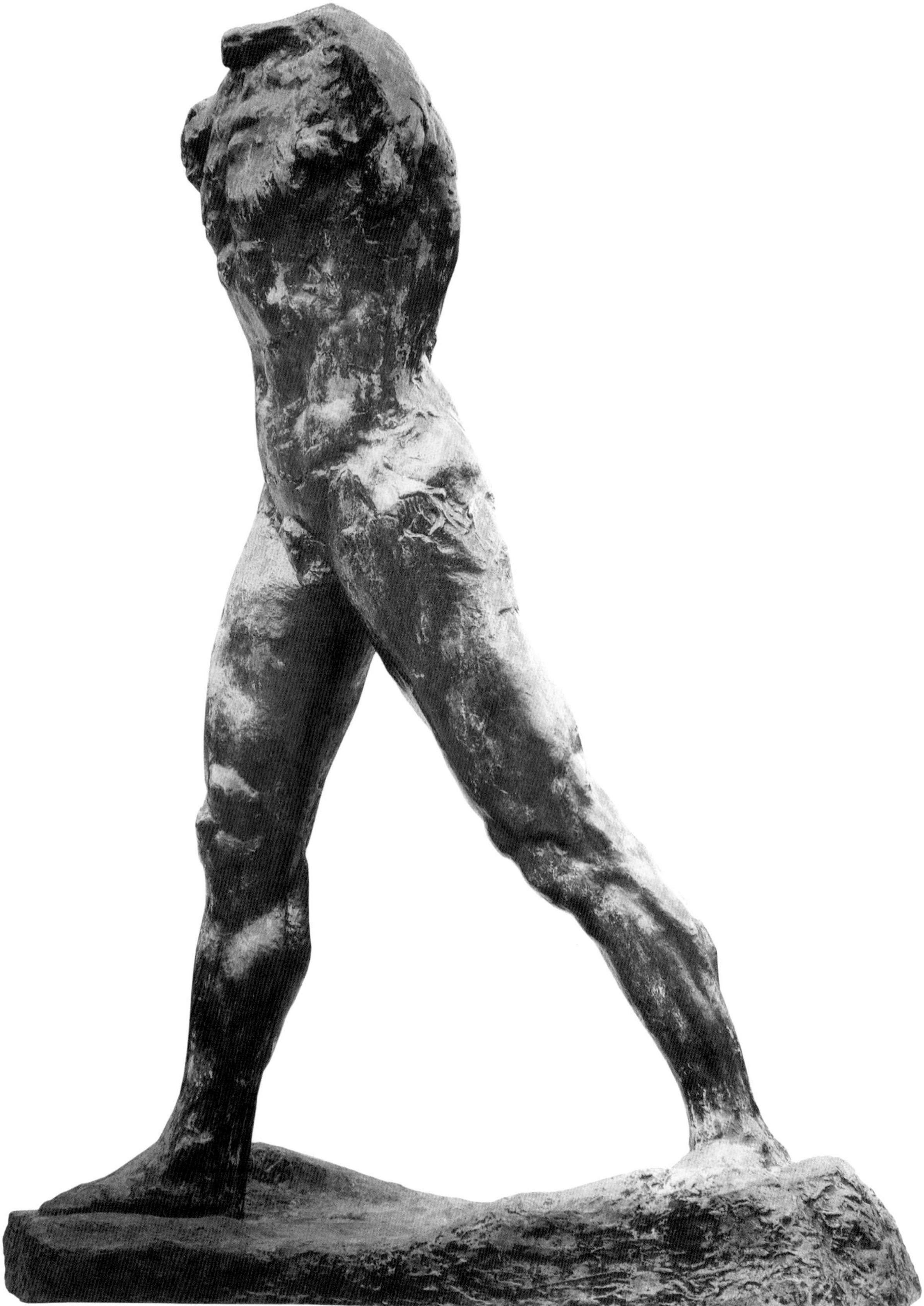

during the modeling of the *Baptist*, was isolated, modified, and subsequently integrated into *The Walking Man* (fig. 17). That Rodin publicly exhibited such fragmentary torsos demonstrated his belief in the self-sufficiency of the partial figure as a vehicle for artistic expression. Implicitly referencing classical artifacts that were universally admired despite being fractured and abraded, the exhibition of these works affirmed Rodin's admiration for classical art while proclaiming his aspiration to rival ancient Greek and Roman masters.

Rodin was impatient with noncreative work, such as enlarging and reducing his sculptures or reproducing compositions in various materials. These tasks were left to assistants or to professionals employed by the foundries where his figures were cast. The demands of creativity, rather than fabrication, were paramount, so he husbanded his time for modeling new works. Feeling that style—and those who stylized—inhibited self-renewal, Rodin was not seduced either by his own virtuosity or by his previous accomplishments. He maintained the detachment to see limitations in what he had done and possessed the imaginative vigor to conceive of alternatives. He saw beginnings where others saw conclusions. Far from rebelling against the tradition of the artist competing for commissions, Rodin boldly attacked the challenges offered by public and private sponsors. They were tests of his originality, inspiring self-surpassing efforts and goading him to push sculpture itself further into areas where it had not been.

While satisfying clients with reproductions of what he had made, Rodin pursued his own vision of what sculpture could be. His willingness to supply the world with large numbers of casts of such favorites as *Eternal Spring* or *The Kiss* (fig. 18)[18] grew out of two interwoven concerns. First, the practice helped maintain the importance of sculpture by encouraging the vogue for various-scaled statuettes, which could be sustained only through the expedient of serial casting (i.e., casting on demand rather than speculatively casting a specific limited edition), and second, proliferation subsidized his extensive atelier and the creation of new works.

Beyond such practical concerns, Rodin was also conscious of living in a time that differed from the past, and he wanted his art to reflect this difference. At the same time he believed that certain aspects of life were timeless and that art should connect the past and present. He frequently credited his audiences with a sophistication they did not always know they had. He was surprised that his candor in addressing what Rilke called the "invisible

17
[OPPOSITE]
The Walking Man, 1878 and 1899–1900, enlarged 1905–7
Cast 1970, 2/12
223.2 × 74.9 × 134.9
1982.306 (cat. 174)

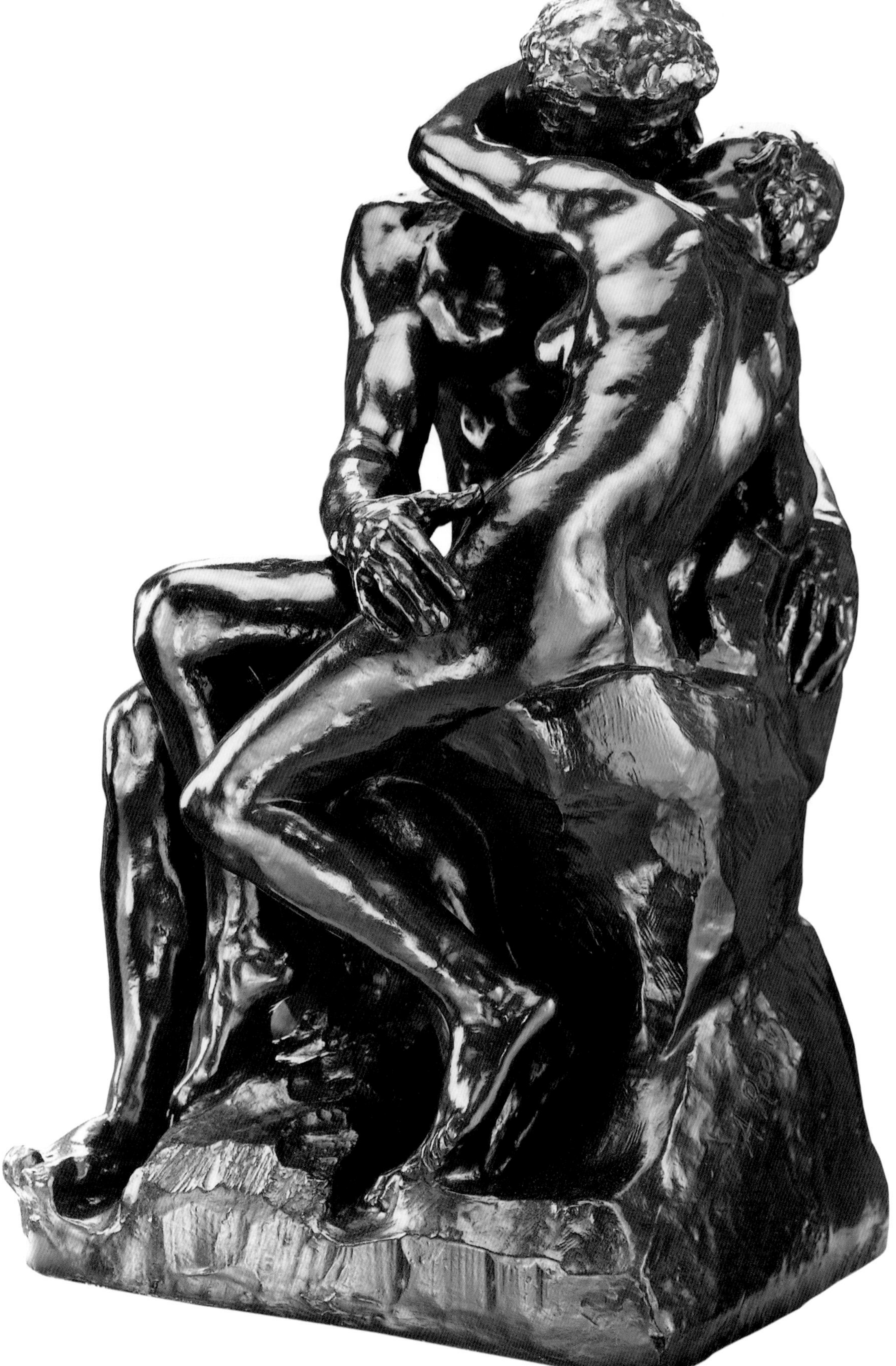

conflicts" of the time shocked his public.[19] Rodin had the courage and patience, however, to impose his vision rather than compromise it. When he collapsed distinctions between what should be shown in public and in private art, he learned to pay the critical price. He bore this cost because his assessment of most other sculpture of his time was that it lacked conviction, truth, and genuine feeling when compared with life.

Rodin's contemporary admirers were enthralled by his art, but otherwise the "master," as they invariably referred to him, may not have been an especially interesting person. His art brought him into contact with many of the most notable people of his era (fig. 19), but with rare exceptions he did not express himself fully in social relations. His profundity lay in his hands, in the discourse of his art, rather than in his words. He was a reformer and revolutionary in art, not in the social sphere; his greatness was in broadening art to include so much of his inner life.

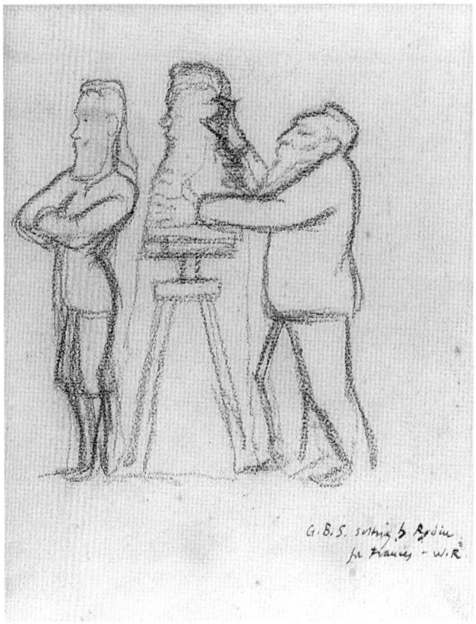

Mastery of Abundance: How Rodin Worked

Rodin inherited a system that enabled a successful sculptor to accommodate great public demand for his work while continuing to engage in new creative efforts. This system presupposed a division of labor and the availability of skilled, specialized technicians. Crucial to his productivity was the establishment during the first half of the nineteenth century of many proficient bronze casting foundries to meet the increasing middle-class demand for cast sculptures. Nevertheless, relatively few of the hundreds of sculptors in Paris in the period from 1870 to 1900 could support themselves fully as independent artists. The Ecole des Beaux-Arts produced wave after wave of sculptors (and painters, of course), but there were just not enough public and private commissions and purchasers to ensure a livelihood for each. Those who did not consistently win major commissions or sell work shown in the great public Salons sought employment with more successful artists.

Rodin could therefore count on a reserve of proficient craftsmen to translate his clay into terra-cotta and plaster, enlarge and reduce his work, construct bases for his sculptures, do carpentry work, build armatures and

18

[OPPOSITE]
The Kiss, c. 1880–81
Cast 1966, 9/12
85.1 × 50.2 × 55.9
1974.36 (cat. 48)

19

[ABOVE]
William Rothenstein (1872–1945)
George Bernard Shaw Posing for Rodin, c. 1906
Chalk
28.2 × 19.2
1988.236 (cat. A51)

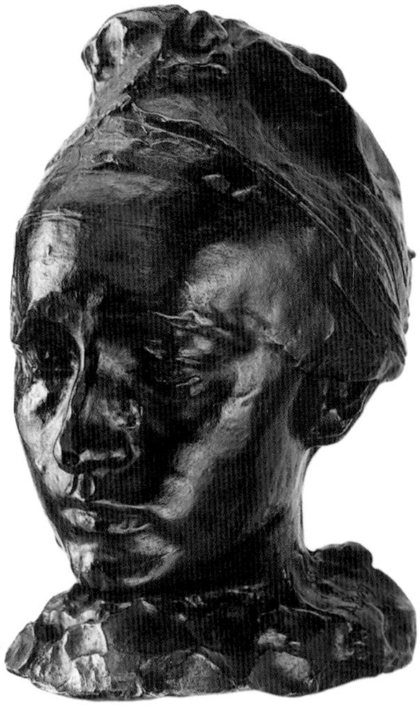

sculpture stands, and transport his larger works between studios and to the railroads. Works in marble were particularly coveted by collectors, and to make them, Rodin employed gifted professionals who carved figures from his plaster or clay maquettes while continuing to exhibit independent works under their own names. As his fame increased, Rodin attracted aspiring sculptors who sought work in his studio, where assisting and studying were essentially synonymous. They came from all over the world. In 1907, for example, the young Romanian sculptor Constantin Brancusi worked for several months in Rodin's studio at Meudon, and over the years, too, the atelier included an unusual number of women, for example, Jeanne Bardey; Camille Claudel (1864–1943; fig. 20), who was particularly adept at modeling hands and feet; and the American Malvina Hoffman.

Rodin and the Photograph

No sculptor before Rodin made as extensive or as imaginative use of photography, and the importance of photographers and journalists in the spread of his influence cannot be overestimated.[20] They gave the sculptor worldwide visibility, which no previous artist in history had experienced. And if that was not enough, Rodin, who never tied himself to any art dealer, enjoyed support from hundreds of self-appointed agents or admirers. The American dancer Loïe Fuller and the Chilean aristocrat Madame Luisa Lynch Morla Vicuña (see fig. 8) were among those who sent him clients from Asia, Europe, and North and South America (fig. 21). At least from the time of the Balzac affair, what Rodin made and exhibited was news from Tokyo to Leningrad to Buenos Aires. Since Rodin's death, only Picasso has known comparable international renown and such broad demand for his work.

From the time of his maturation as a sculptor in the late 1870s, Rodin had recourse to the camera: first, to record his work and, later, to reflect his own vision of art and the human form. Although he seems never to have taken a photograph himself, Rodin trained several gifted photographers to be his surrogates, to see his work in depth and atmosphere, while he also encouraged their own interpretation and development. We know that in many cases the sculptor directed the lighting and composition for his photographers, so that we can see his work, often in the spaces where it was made,

20
[ABOVE]
Portrait of Camille Claudel in a Bonnet, 1885–86
Cast 1969, 7/12
25.4 × 14 × 15.2
1974.77 (cat. 90)

21
[OPPOSITE]
Maquette for "Monument to General Lynch," 1886
Cast 1973, 3/12
43.8 × 22.9 × 13.3
1975.85 (cat. 7)

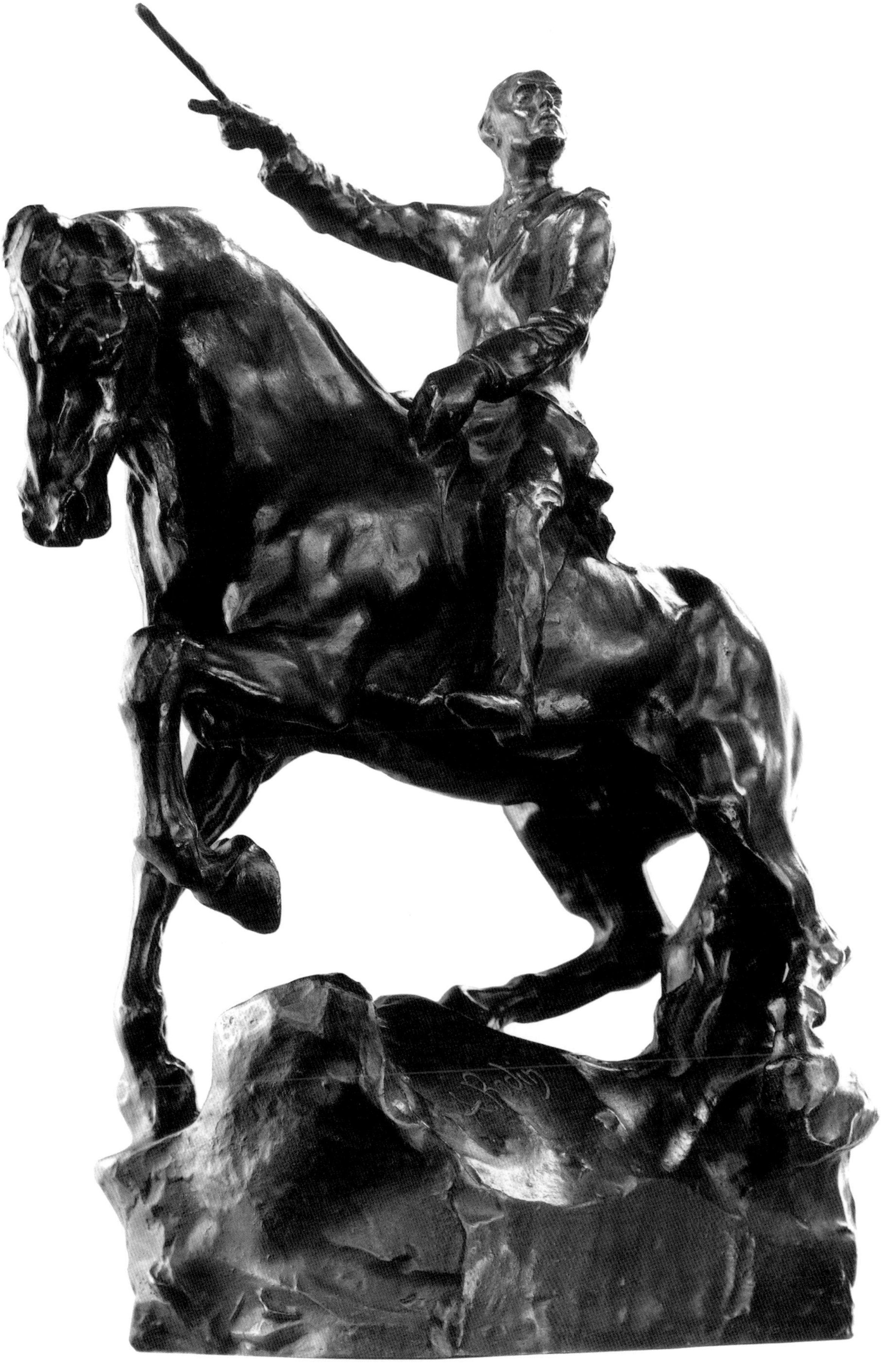

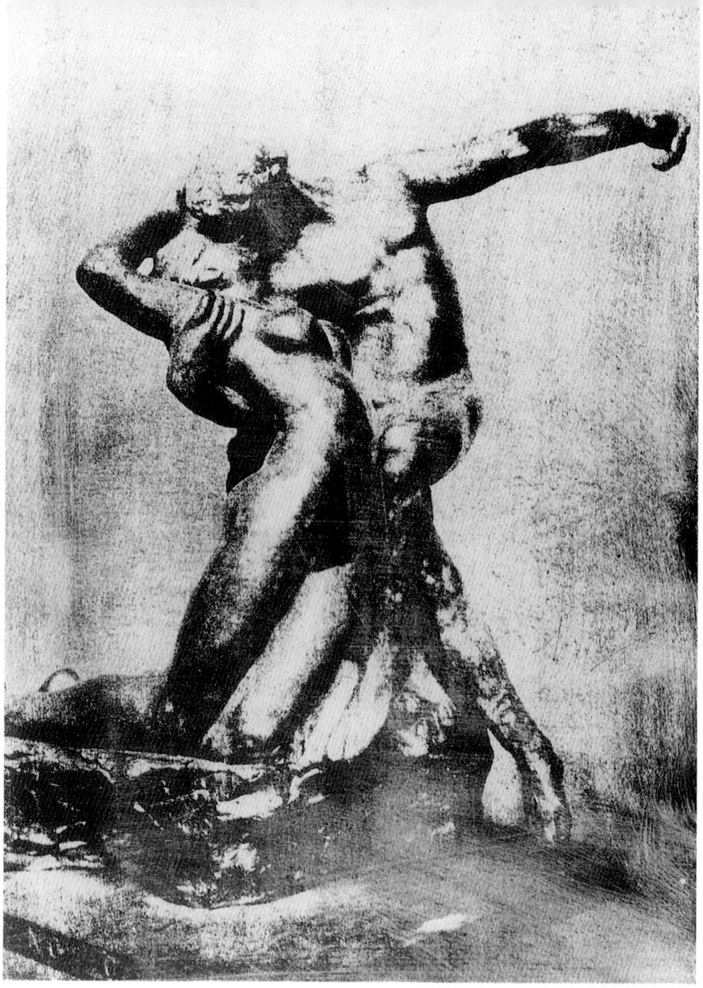

22
[RIGHT]
Jean-François Limet (1855–1941)
Eternal Springtime in Bronze, 1900–1915
Gum bichromate print
39 × 29.5
1978.71.2a (cat. A153, recto)

23
[OPPOSITE]
Edward Steichen (1879–1973)
Balzac—the Open Sky, 1908
Photogravure
20.7 × 15.8
Gift of the William Rubin Foundation,
1974.233.1 (cat. A161)

from the point of view and under the illumination that he thought best served his intent.

It is not surprising that photographs did much to establish Rodin's reputation in his lifetime. As the foremost international representative of advanced art, Rodin allowed himself to become a subject for talented, innovative photographers such as Gertrude Käsebier. In the retrospective he organized for himself in 1900, Rodin allowed the photographer Eugène Druet to exhibit for sale a roomful of his photographs of Rodin's sculpture.[21] Other photographers, such as Jean-François Limet, created artistically manipulated gum bichromate prints that dramatize the sculptures (fig. 22). Introduced to Rodin through reports of the Balzac controversy in a Milwaukee newspaper, the young Edward Steichen traveled to Paris especially to meet Rodin. There Steichen made inspired photographs that simultaneously affirmed the attributes of the *Monument to Honoré de Balzac* that had offended academicians and helped to reveal its awesome grandeur to an international audience when they were published in Alfred Stieglitz's influential periodical *Camera Work* (fig. 23).[22]

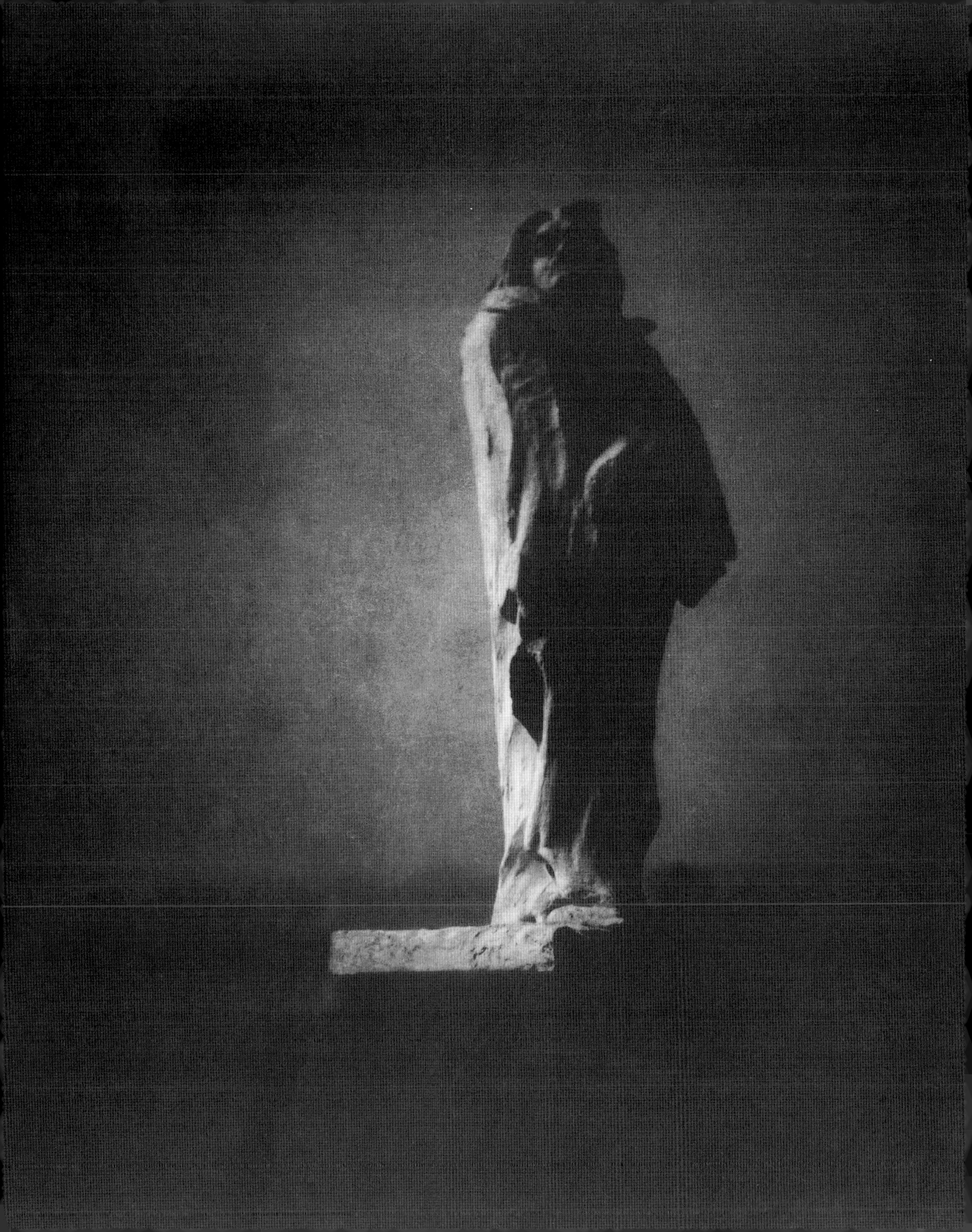

Reproducing Rodin: Enlargements, Reductions, and Alternative Media

Until 1882 Rodin was obliged to work for other artists in order to support himself, his family, and at least one assistant. While he lived and worked in Belgium from 1870 to 1877, he made some "pastries," that is, commercially attractive heads such as *Suzon*, which were reproduced in unlimited editions. By the 1870s in France and Belgium, a bronze or a sculpture in any medium was seen by the middle class as a status symbol, and often they were given for wedding presents. In Paris, Rodin contracted with the Leblanc–Barbedienne foundry to cast unlimited editions of *The Kiss* and *Eternal Springtime* in sizes that the foundry deemed commercially attractive. The Cantor Arts Center's small gilt bronze *Kiss* is such a cast.[23] Periodically Rodin received an accounting and royalties on the sales of his work.

In 1895 Rodin contracted with another foundry to reproduce in large quantity plaster casts of his popular *Bust of Victor Hugo*. Rodin seems to have had relatively inexpensive wax casts made of some of his works, such as his *Bust of Henri Rochefort*, to sell or to give to friends (fig. 24). Stanford's green wax cast of Rochefort suggests bronze, while yellow wax casts Rodin made of his *Bust of Mrs. Russell* (1888), for example, could be mistaken for marble. The ceramic *Bust of Jean d'Aire* (fig. 25) is one of several works that

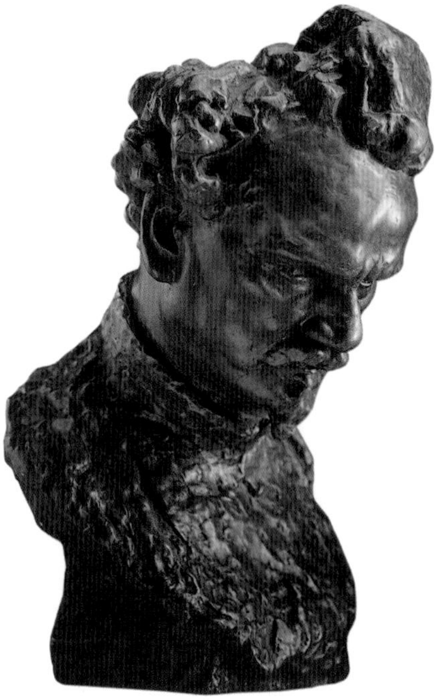

24
[ABOVE]
Bust of Henri Rochefort, 1884
Wax cast
37.5 × 21.6 × 19.4
1977.16 (cat. 134)

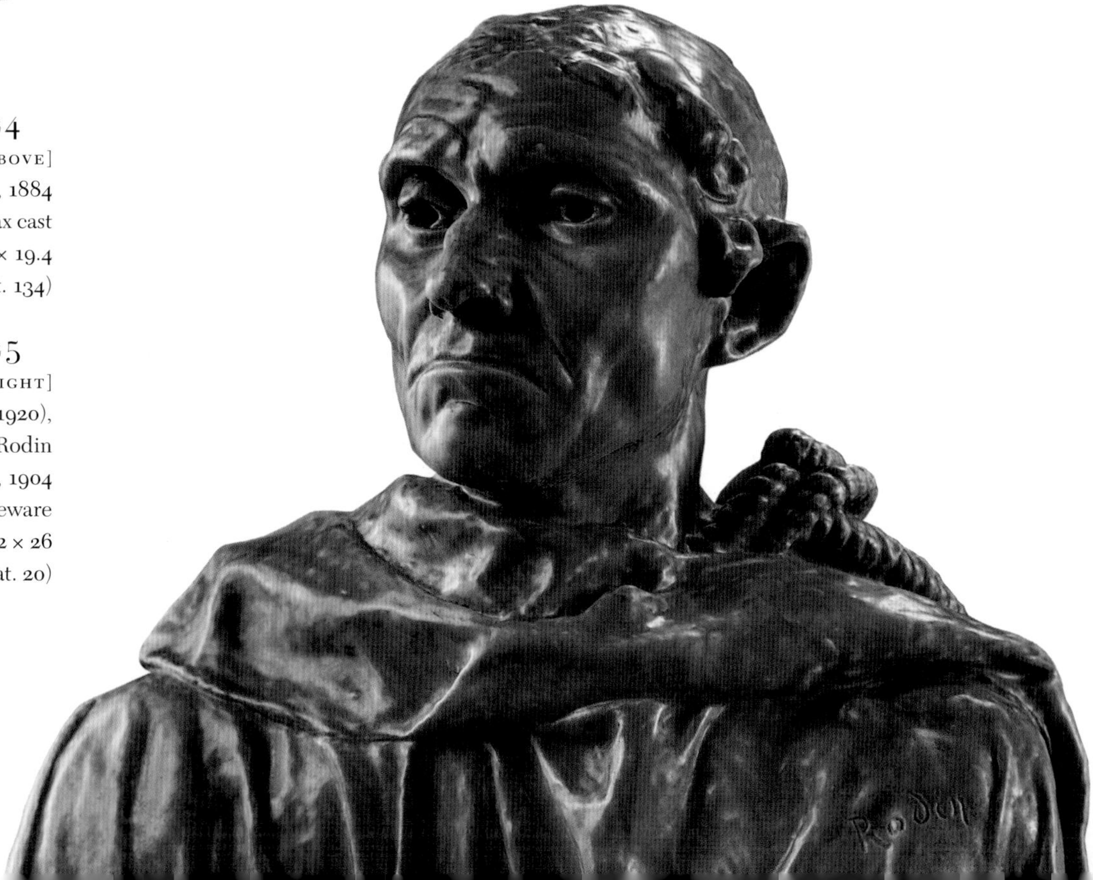

25
[RIGHT]
Paul Jeanneney (1861–1920),
after Auguste Rodin
Bust of Jean d'Aire, 1904
Stoneware
45.7 × 52 × 26
1974.87 (cat. 20)

he commissioned from the ceramist Paul Jeanneney (1861–1920), whose signature appears on the Stanford cast along with that of the sculptor.[24] Ceramic casts enabled Rodin to explore a greater range of surface color (an interest he shared with contemporaries who also sought to expand sculpture's potential). In addition, ceramic casts were less expensive than bronzes or marbles, but like them, they could also be shown out of doors.

To meet the worldwide demand for reduced versions of his sculpture, Rodin availed himself of an ancient process, called "pointing," that had been mechanized in the nineteenth century. Greek sculptors had reduced or enlarged their works by hand, by means of a series of mathematical proportions applied to a selected series of points on the model to be reproduced. Using the tip of the nose and a point on the chin, for example, a head could be enlarged by doubling or tripling the distance between these two points. Through the early nineteenth century, assistants would rough out the reproduction, and presumably the master sculptor would finish it. In 1834 the French engineer Achille Collas patented a device that facilitated the process. The model to be reduced was placed on one turntable, and a "blank" of clay or soft plaster was placed on a second turntable connected to the first (fig. 26). Using a stylus linked to a sharp cutting tool, the reproducer would trace all of the model's profiles. The cutting tool, because of its link to the stylus, would simultaneously cut the same profiles, enlarged or reduced, into the "blank." As the model was turned, so was the "blank." The reproducer would work first broadly and then more finely until all of the excess clay or plaster had been removed. The resulting reproduction might be finished by hand if necessary.

From at least 1894 until his death, Rodin's most trusted reproducer was Henri Lebossé, a trained sculptor and son of a reproducer. He not only reduced *The Age of Bronze*, *John the Baptist*, and five of the six individual Burghers of Calais, but he also enlarged such important sculptures as the monument to Balzac and *The Thinker*. Rodin's use of the Collas method for enlarging important works to their final scale seems to have been unusual, and he may have been the first artist to do so. With more complex figures such as *The Thinker*, Lebossé would enlarge in clay a single limb, which would then be cast in plaster by one of Rodin's assistants. When all of the parts were done, they would be assembled (fig. 27).

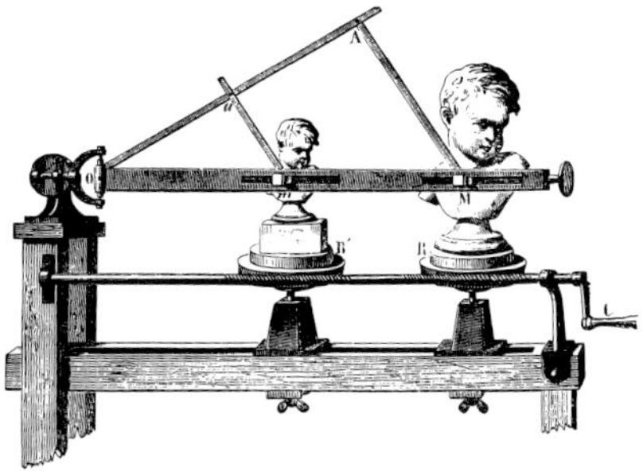

26
[ABOVE]
Collas sculpture-reducing machine
From Paul Poiré, *La France industrielle*
(Paris: Hachette, 1880)

27
[BELOW]
Photographer unknown
Plaster expert Paul Cruet attaching head to enlargement of *Ugolino and His Sons*, c. 1911
Collection Marion Angell Boyer and Francis Boyer Library, Philadelphia Museum of Art

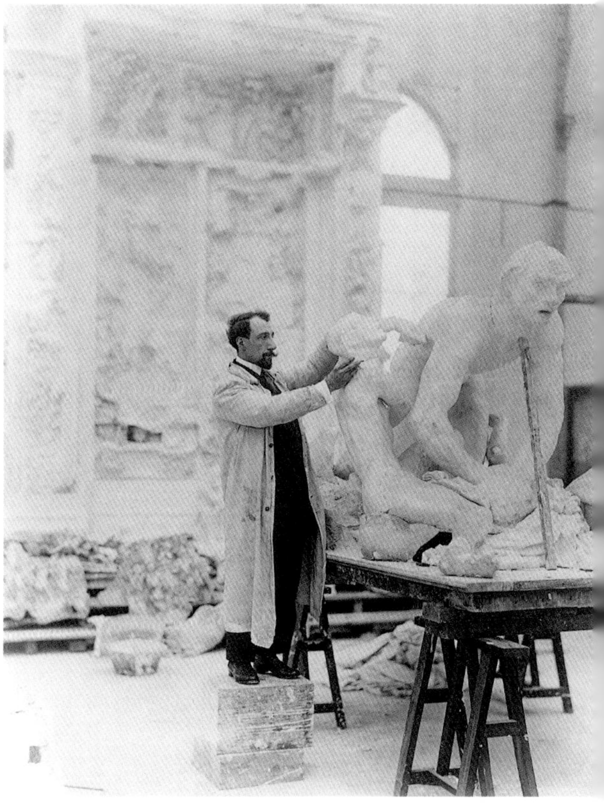

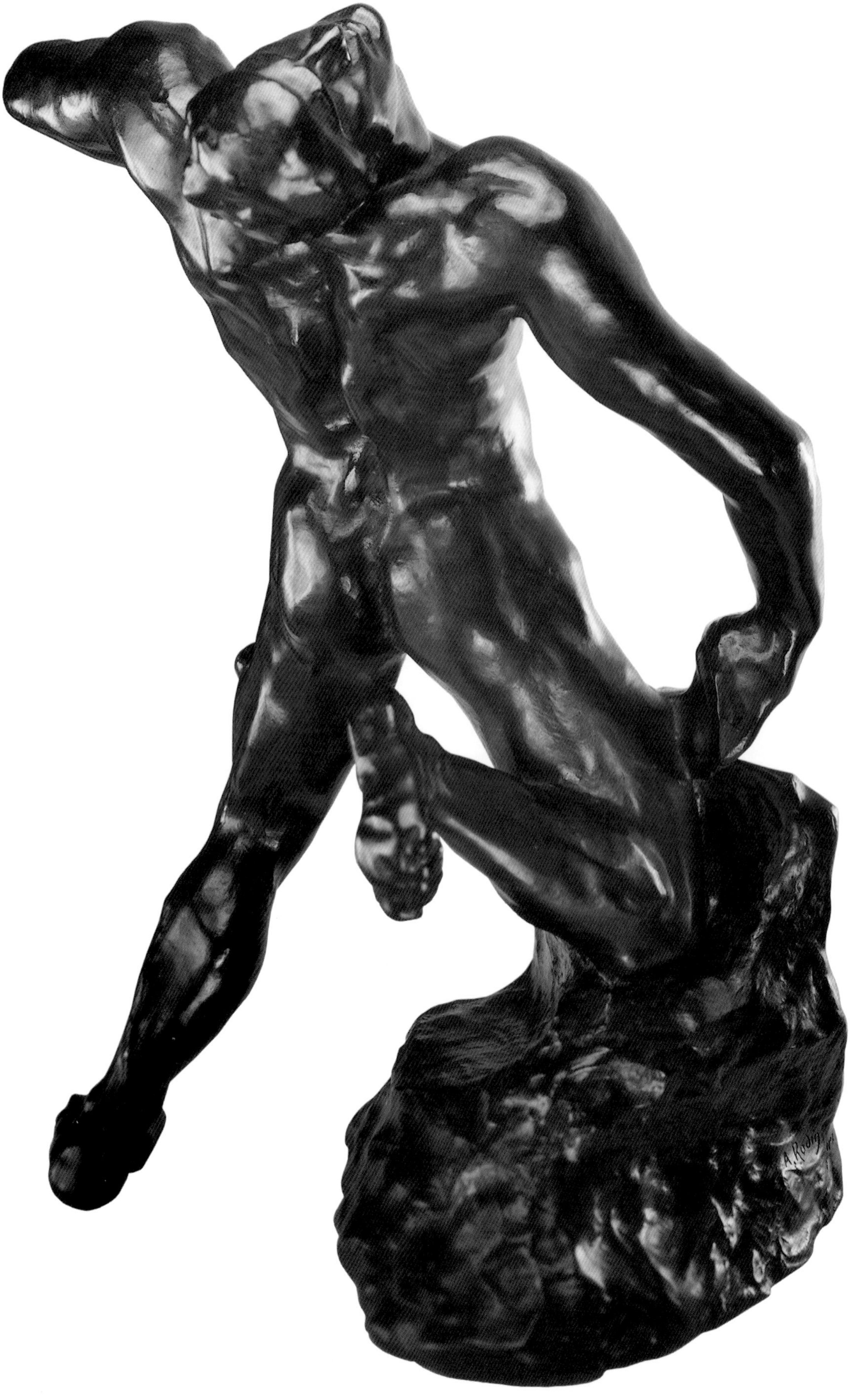

This process was far from being a purely mechanical means of reproduction, which Rodin detested. We know from Lebossé's notes to Rodin that many judgments were made and changes introduced during the process. While it appears that Rodin's custom was to permit Lebossé to complete the work in clay, he followed the process closely and imposed tough standards. Moreover, Rodin sometimes intervened by editing the plasters prior to casting. Lebossé's work for Rodin was public knowledge and was accepted by the artist's clients. For his part, Lebossé was proud of his skill at reproducing Rodin's ideas and his distinctive "touch," of being the sculptor's "perfect collaborator," but he never claimed coauthorship of the works he reproduced, as they were derived entirely from Rodin's plaster models.[25]

A Sculpture Is Never Finished

Genius loves frugality. Rodin did not let a good sculptural idea go to waste or limit it to one appearance in his art. For example, *The Falling Man* (fig. 28) appears twice on *The Gates of Hell* (figs. 29, 30) and was exhibited as an independent figure, coupled with a woman in the composition *I Am Beautiful*, and in other combinations and variants, including as a limbless torso.[26] In the 1890s Rodin became increasingly daring in his use of partial figures and in juxtaposing divergent elements to create provocative new

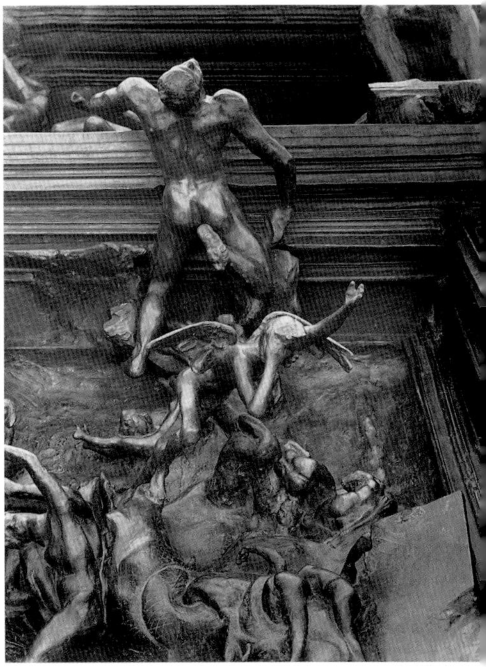

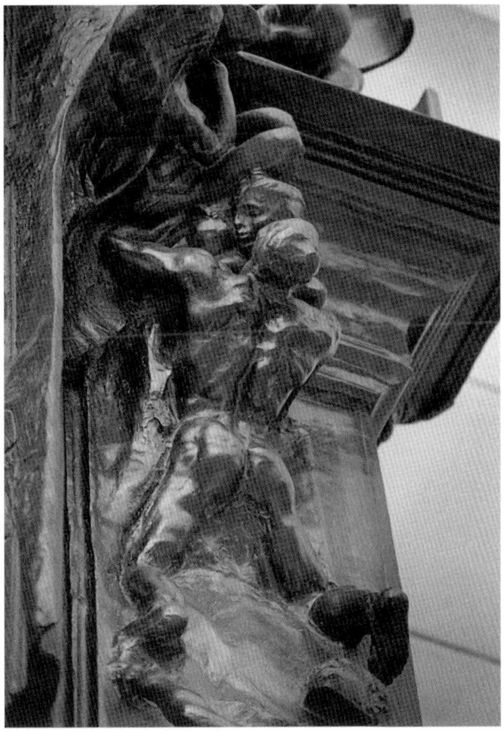

28
[OPPOSITE]
The Falling Man, 1882
Cast 1978, 7/12
53.2 × 42.5 × 29.8
1992.139 (cat. 64)

29
[FAR RIGHT]
Detail of *The Gates of Hell* with *The Falling Man*

30
[RIGHT]
Detail of *The Gates of Hell* with *The Falling Man* in the group *I Am Beautiful*

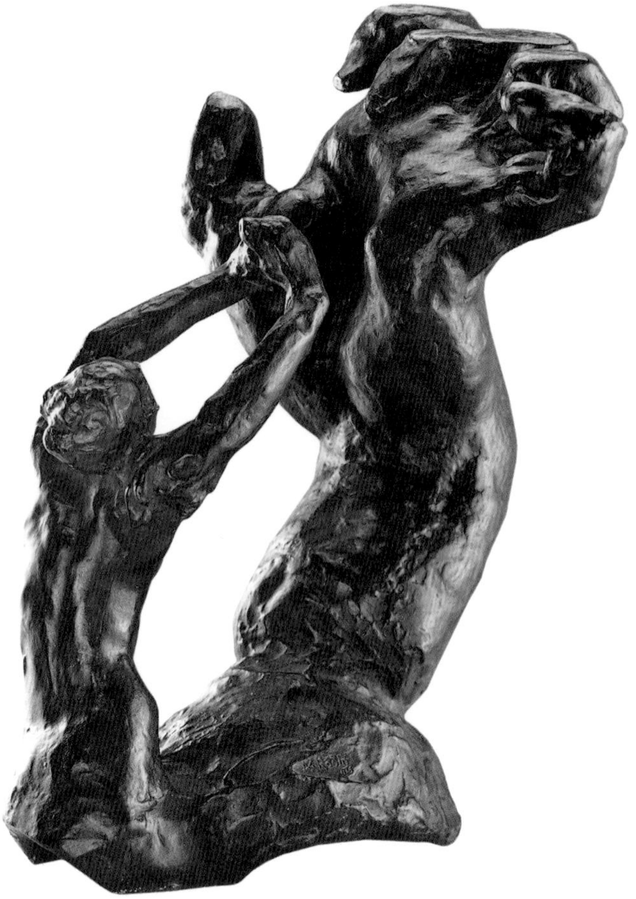

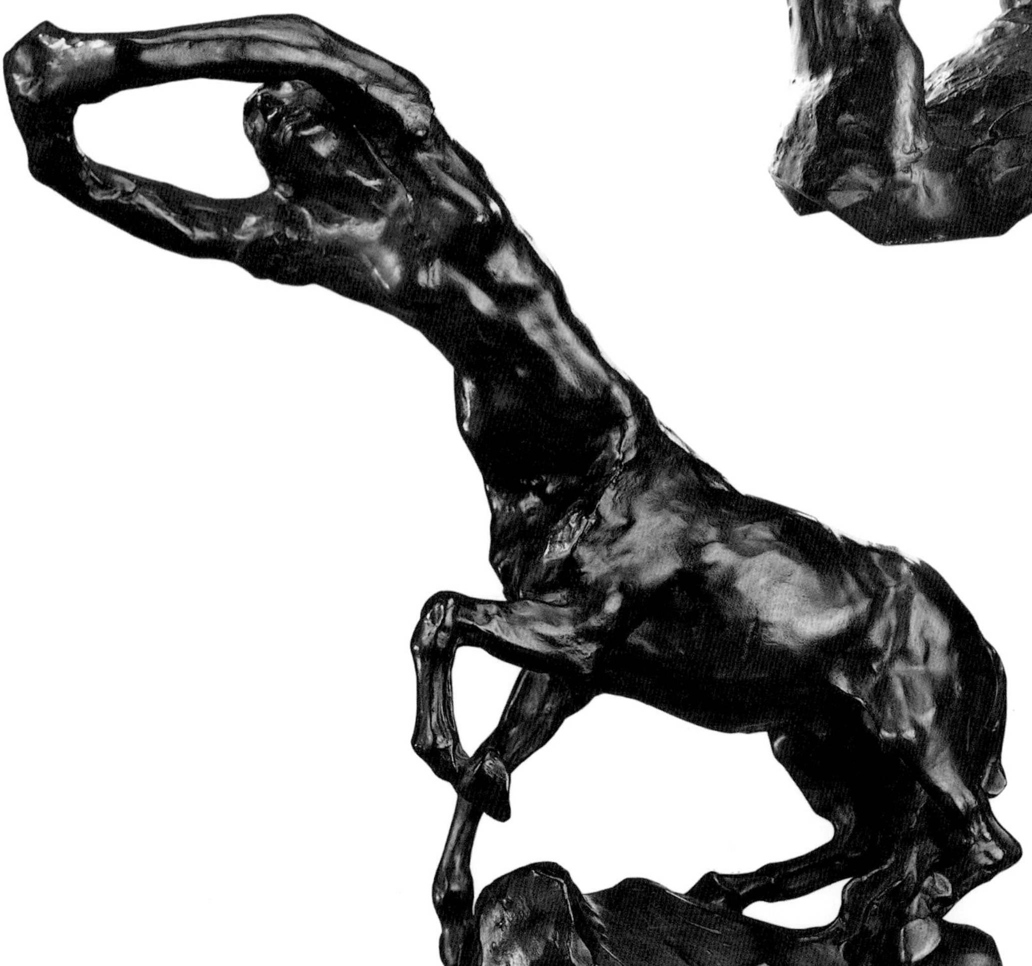

assemblages.[27] One result of such experimentation, *Large Clenched Left Hand with Figure* (fig. 31), can be "deconstructed" to examine this facet of Rodin's creative process. His partial figure called *Imploring Woman* (also called *Despairing Adolescent*) was itself a hybrid of parts assembled from previous works. The head, which seems to be derived from one of the sons of Ugolino on *The Gates of Hell*, and the arms and torso all had previous histories. Rodin had joined them in the motif of *Imploring Woman*, which was then joined with one of his expressive studies of a hand. He similarly joined a plaster of *Imploring Woman* with the body of the horse from his model for the unrealized equestrian monument to General Patricio Lynch (see fig. 21) to create *The Centauress* (fig. 32).

As can be seen in this figure, Rodin did not always hide the joining of disparate motifs. On the contrary, by not reworking the juncture, he emphasized rather than disguised the creative process itself, which in turn enriched its meaning. Truman Bartlett saw Rodin's composite creature as yearning despairingly, "an image of the soul, whose heavenly impulses rest miserably captive to the bodily clay." Rodin responded that such works "awaken the imagination of the spectators" and "give rein to roam at will." He concluded: "That is, according to me, the role of art. The form which it creates ought only to furnish a pretext for the unlimited development of emotion."[28] Rodin's grafting process reminds us that he did much of his work not in the presence of the living model—the method for which he was so famous—but in private, his imagination stimulated by his own art. For Rodin, art was a continuum interrupted only by death.

31
[OPPOSITE TOP]
Large Clenched Left Hand with Figure, c. 1890 or c. 1907
Cast 1972, 6/12
45.7 × 30.5 × 26.7
1974.47 (cat. 193)

32
[OPPOSITE BOTTOM]
The Centauress, c. 1887
Cast 1969, 3/12
40 × 45.1 × 17.8
1974.57 (cat. 158)

33
[BELOW]
Bust of Saint John the Baptist, 1878
Cast 1968, 3/12
55.9 × 38.1 × 25.4
1974.65 (cat. 131)

Giving a Face to History and Myth: Rodin's Heads and Portraits

Rodin produced a large number of powerful heads. Many were actual portraits, and others have a portraitlike quality but were destined to surmount biblical, mythological, or allegorical figures when not shown independently. For example, he exhibited his *Bust of Saint John the Baptist* (fig. 33) in 1879, one year before the full figure was first shown. To re-create a biblical personage in the act of announcing Christ's coming, he had to invent what his model's face could not give him. Studies for it indicate that Rodin came slowly to the

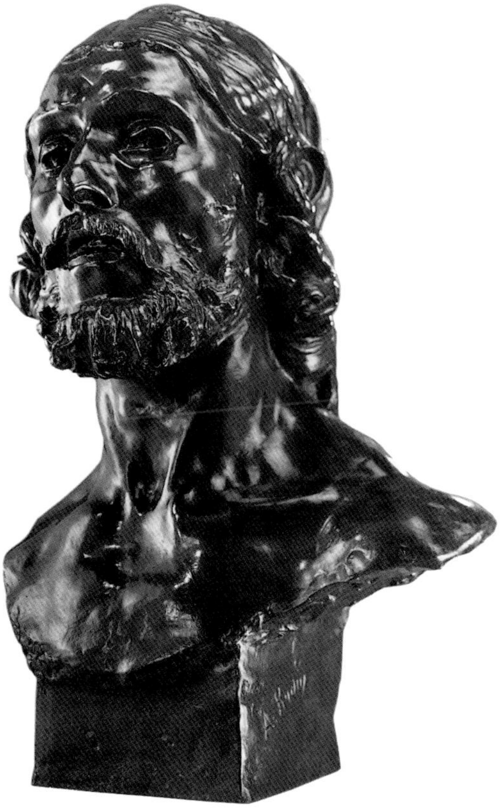

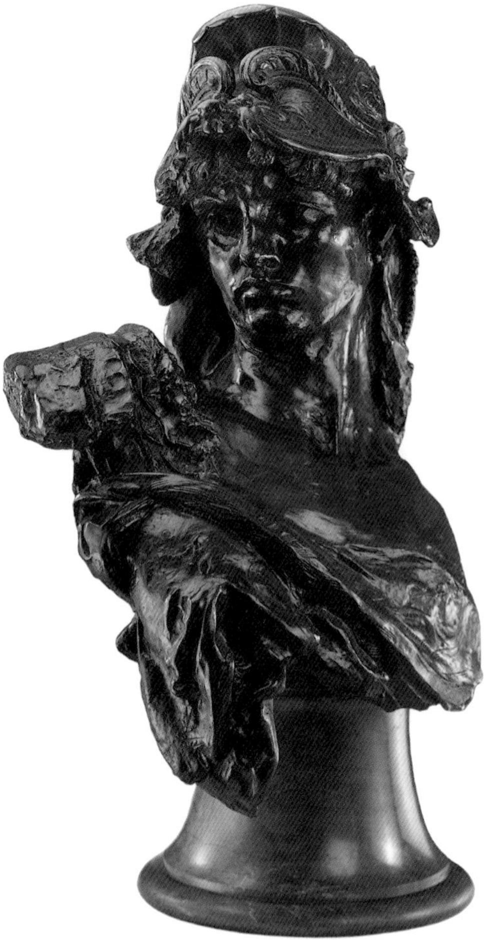

34
[RIGHT]
Bellona, 1878–79
A. Gruet foundry, c. 1893
78.7 × 47 × 45.1
1974.63 (cat. 5)

35
[BELOW]
The Tempest, 1886(?)
Cast c. 1903
34.9 × 29.8 × 27.9
1974.69 (cat. 143)

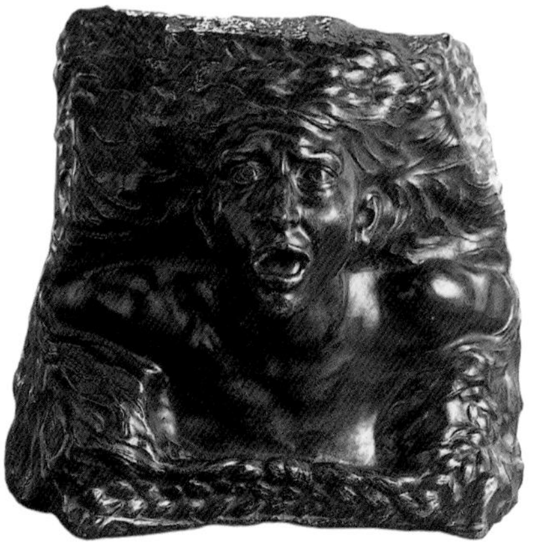

definition of both its features and its expression. Rodin's *Bellona* (fig. 34), the Roman goddess of war, however, was reportedly inspired by the angry face of his lifelong mistress, Rose, during one of their arguments. This is the finest bronze cast in Stanford's collection and dates from the artist's lifetime. The magnificent helmet, which was inspired by those of Michelangelo's helmeted Medici dukes (Medici Chapel, San Lorenzo, Florence), was modeled by one of Rodin's many talented assistants, Auguste Ladrou (1860–1902), who specialized in decorative sculpture. *Bellona* served Rodin unsuccessfully in a competition for a monument to the Third French Republic, and it was also exhibited with the names of heroic women such as Clorinda from Torquato Tasso's *Jerusalem Delivered*. Throughout his career the titles Rodin gave his sculptures were as flexible as his plaster subjects, serving to expand the realm of possible meanings that might be evoked by a composition.

It was Rodin's practice after about 1880 first to make an expressive head or figure and then let it suggest titles to himself or others. *The Tempest* (fig. 35), first created about 1886, was variously titled *The Runner of Marathon*,

The Wind, and *The Terror*. Known also in two marble versions for which no architectural or other context has been identified, the relief—with its wild-eyed and thrusting, open-mouthed face—demonstrates Rodin's absolute mastery of expressive physiognomy. This ability is nowhere more powerfully enacted than in his humanization of the mythical muse. In his *Head of the Tragic Muse* (fig. 36), destined for his ill-fated *Monument to Victor Hugo*, Rodin's muse is not a passive bearer of divine inspiration; rather she takes on the anguish of the artist. The distortion of this tormented head was achieved not just by an exaggerated psychological depiction, but by the sculptor slamming his left hand into the right side of the clay head. In his heads of Iris (figs. 37, 38), Rodin took audacious liberties, challenging the traditional limits of form to achieve an untranslatable expression that in the enlarged version verges on a type of chaos.

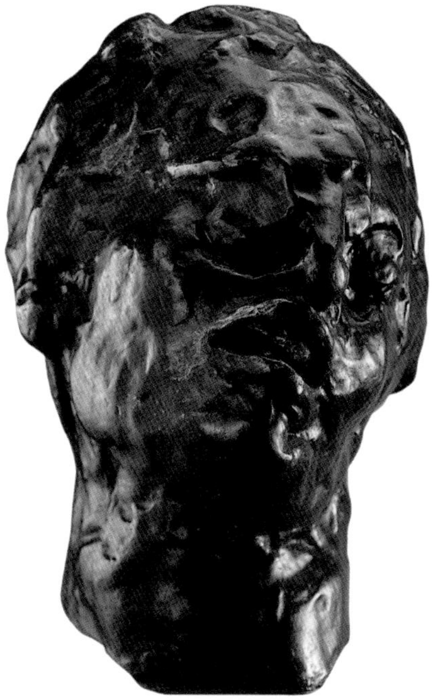

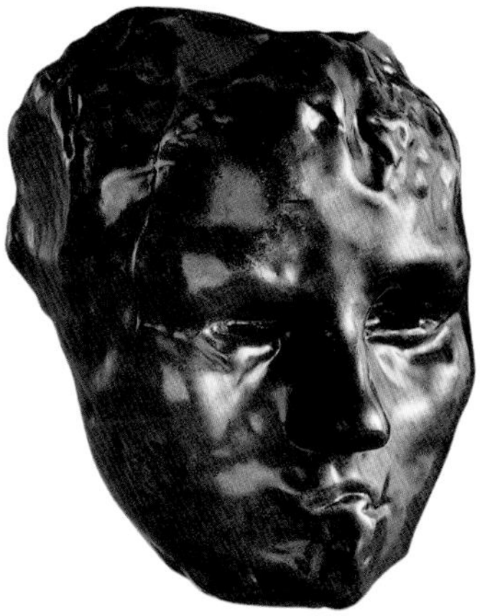

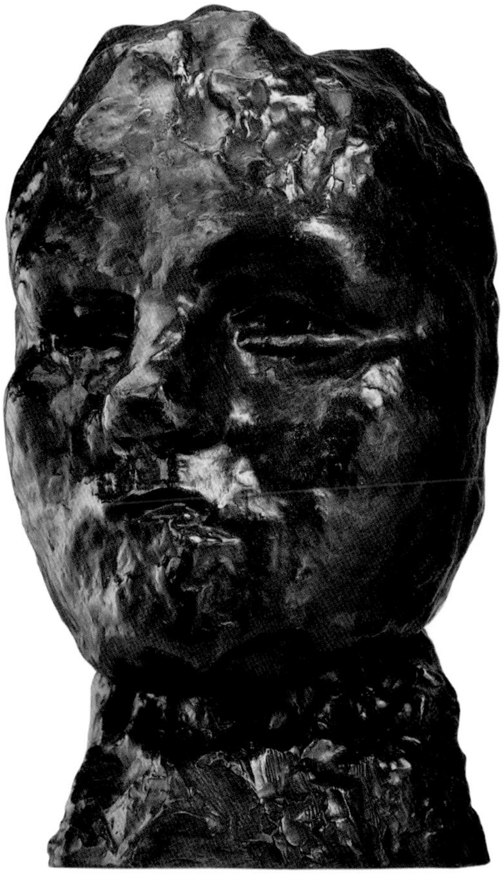

36
[ABOVE]
Head of the Tragic Muse, c. 1893–96
Cast 1973, 1/12
28.9 × 18.1 × 23
1974.84 (cat. 88)

37
[FAR LEFT]
Head of Iris, c. 1890
Cast 1969, 1/12
19.1 × 12.7 × 16.5
1974.85 (cat. 139)

38
[LEFT]
Monumental Head of Iris, c. 1890, enlarged 1898(?)
Cast 1970, 7/12
61 × 33 × 33
1974.64 (cat. 140)

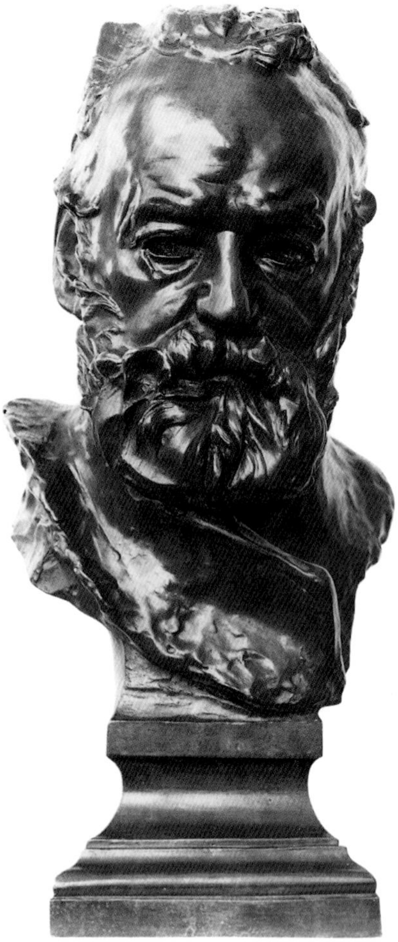

During the 1880s in particular, Rodin produced a multitude of actual portraits (fig. 39), some made on commission for the socially prominent and many others made as gifts for patrons and friends. Speaking in 1913 to Henri-Charles-Etienne Dujardin-Beaumetz, the undersecretary of state for fine arts, Rodin explained that he invariably found these works very challenging: "You will never fully believe what tenacity it takes to make a bust and how hard one must fight to find and render a true character within it, accentuating and emphasizing the solid, supple, ample, and free form." A bust, he continued, "is the sea with its movements, its high waves and their depths. As on the sea, when one works, one climbs up, sinks down, believes himself lost, yet rises again and makes port.... Sometimes I have started a single bust over again ten times. Thus I have made multiple aspects and diverse expressions of it; at the end, what joy to see and understand! Wishing to do better, one sometimes demolishes even what one has done well; but one must be possessed by the demon of the best." Rodin concluded that "a beautiful bust shows the model in his moral and physical reality, tells his secret thoughts, sounds the inmost recesses of his soul, his greatnesses, his weaknesses; all the masks fall off.... Through his own sensibility, the artist becomes a revealer, a diviner.... When he has looked, composed, and followed with sincerity all the indications of truth in transmitting them to clay."[29]

Less Is More: The Partial Figure

Rodin's most important contribution to future sculptors was the partial figure. He established a new premise for sculpture by demonstrating that a complete work of art, as opposed to an anatomically whole or academically finished sculpture, need not show the entire human form. As precedents he cited not only the history of portrait busts but also ancient fragments, which, though reduced to a fragmentary state by the accidents of time, nevertheless revealed, through an aesthetic synecdoche, the beauty and perfection of the whole. Rodin created partial figures all of his artistic life: as preliminary studies for statues, after the fact as fragmented forms of full figures, or simply as études of a body part, such as a torso or hand (figs. 40, 41). It was his conviction that he could impart the expressiveness of the human face to any and all parts of the human body. Many of his fragmented forms still bear the raw marks of their editing or unmaking, so that there is a confluence of illusionism: the imitation of nature and the artifice of art.

39
[ABOVE]
Bust of Victor Hugo, 1883
J. Petermann foundry, 1883
57.2 × 26.6 × 27.9
Gift of Cyril Magnin,
1971.5 (cat. 86)

40
[OPPOSITE]
Torso of a Young Woman,
1886, enlarged 1908–9
Cast 1960, 10/12
84.4 × 49.5 × 31.7
Gift of the Ahmanson Trust,
1981.323 (cat. 177)

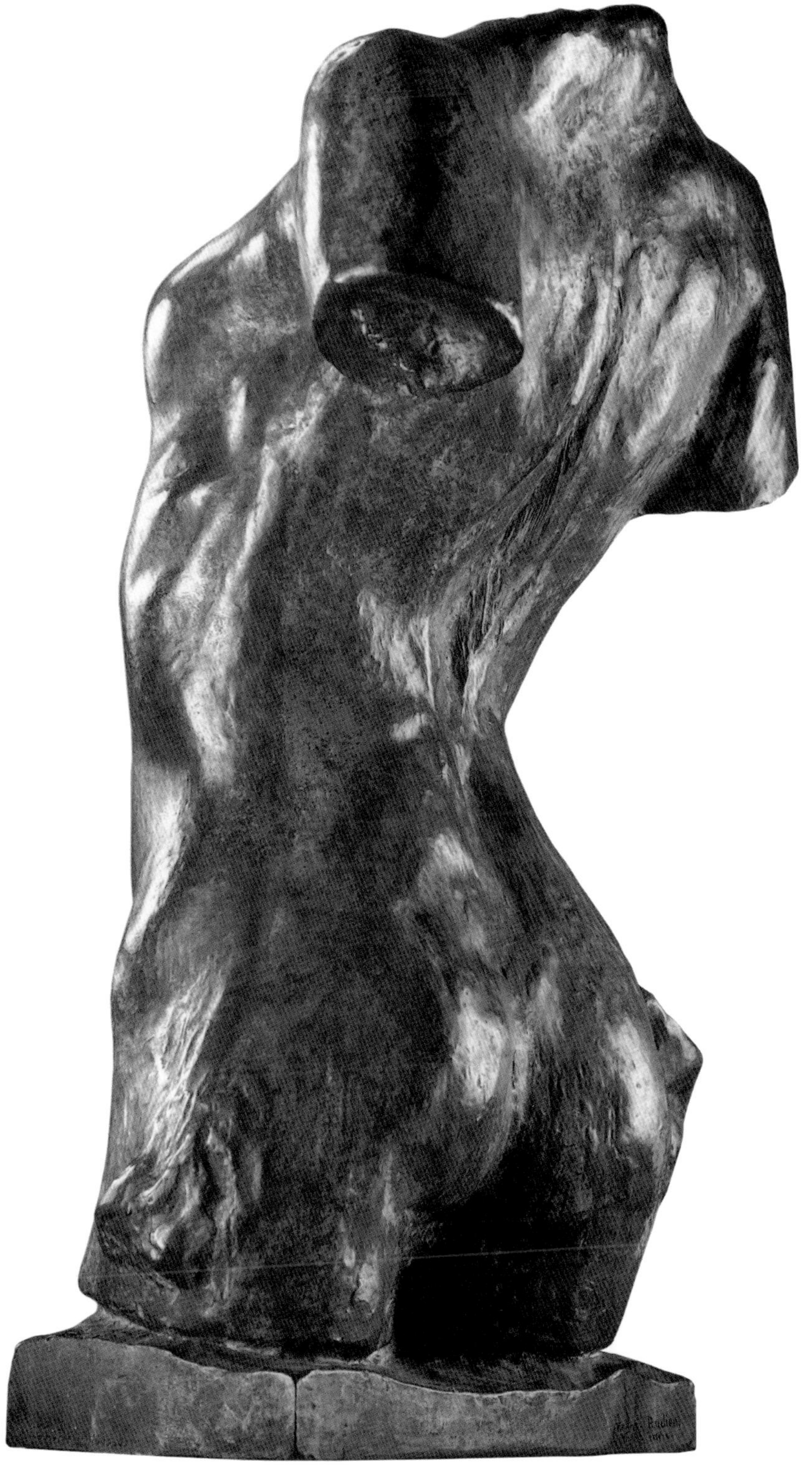

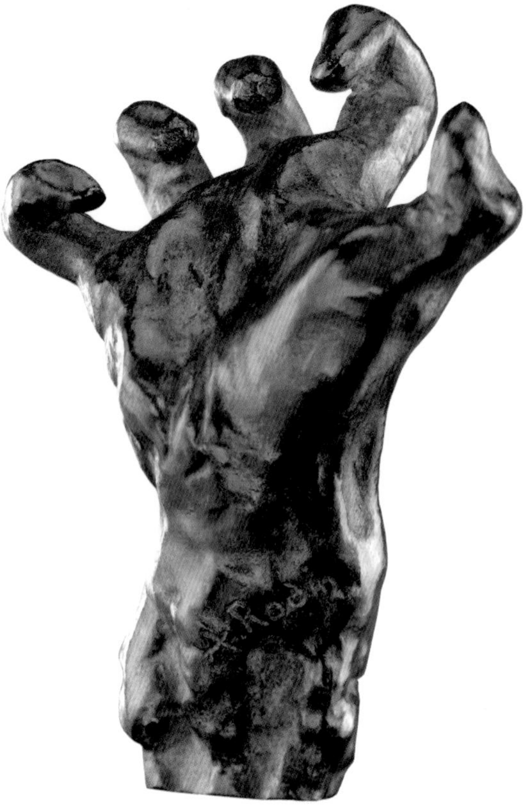

41
Small Clenched Right Hand, 1884–89(?)
Alexis Rudier foundry
13.7 × 10.3 × 19.8
1978.124 (cat. 188)

Through the partial figure Rodin sought to draw attention to the beauties of modeling and the mysteries of métier. Shorn of heads or hands, his partial figures are cut off from history and culture. Conventional rhetoric and traditional iconography were set aside, yet he did not create abstractions. Following a visit to Rodin's studio in 1888, the writer Rodolphe Darzens concluded, "Rodin does not capture gesture alone—he sets in stone the fleeting, almost elusive character of thought . . . and makes us believe in the possibility of a soul, palpitating in the depths of the clay."[30] Each fragment the sculptor modeled affirms life and manifests the passions of the spirit. After 1900, through his partial figures even more than through his full-length sculptures, Rodin renewed himself and his art in pursuit of new formal adventure. Looking at them through the filter of twentieth-century abstract sculpture, we can see what was obscure to Rodin's contemporaries: with his partial figures Rodin achieved compelling artistic forms unpredictable on the basis of our knowledge of the body. The largest display of his partial figures took place in 1900, during his retrospective in Paris. Then and thereafter criticism of this aspect of his art was strongest and earned for the sculptor the reputation of a sadist, pervert, mystifier, and cheat who withheld his full talent from the public.

One of those closest to Rodin after 1900 was Judith Cladel. In the first edition of her biography of the sculptor, published in 1908, she illuminated the criticism, Rodin's response to it, and, most important, the value and purpose of his partial figures:

> The master has exhibited his *morceaux* (fragments) and they have evoked from his critics the rudest criticism. These critics have never wanted to comprehend that he has not delivered to them works that were properly decorative but were rather the unique beauty of métier which appear here more thrilling than in his more finished sculptures. . . . Nothing veils or covers them, neither the interest of the subject, nor the expression of sentiment or feeling. All that is there is the quality of modeling, the raw result of work. In reality it is not Iris, The Earth, The Muse, but torsos which appear to be fragments of a destroyed movement: It is the sum of art, a certificate that the sculptor gives himself the total of his efforts and researches concentrated in plastic formulas. Therefore, of what importance is it to him to achieve details or a seductive arrangement? Who contemplates these works must do it with the *esprit de savant* before a morceau of nature to be studied and not with the attitude of a dilettante looking for esthetic pleasure and the emotion of the subject that does not exist. Like an historian, Rodin names them his essays, and they are truly pages from the history of his art. The misunderstanding that they establish between the public and the artist is enormous. The crowds having lost the sense of the value of modeling, take Rodin for a mystifier, obstinately or perversely cutting off the limbs of his statues. I have heard a young sculptor announce with the serene conviction of a fool, "This year I exhibited the body of a woman à la Rodin. I squarely cut off the arms and legs."[31]

In conversation with the artist Michel Georges-Michel around 1912, Rodin described his trials with exhibiting the partial figure and provided an additional explanation of why he made them: "Have not the public and critics who serve the public reproached me enough for exhibiting simple parts of the human body? . . . These people comprehend nothing of sculpture, or what is an étude. They cannot imagine that an artist must apply himself to giving as much expression to a hand or a torso as to a face and that it was logical for an artist to exhibit an arm rather than a 'bust' arbitrarily deprived by tradition of arms, legs, and abdomen. Expression and proportion, the ends are there. The means are modeling. It is by modeling that flesh lives, vibrates, struggles and suffers."[32] Demonstrating that the partial figure could be complete as a work of art was one of Rodin's greatest legacies to subsequent sculptors. Rilke recognized this in 1903, when he wrote in his brilliant essay on the sculptor that "an artistic whole need not necessarily coincide with the complete thing. . . . In the art of sculpture . . . it is left to the artist to make out of many things one thing, and from the smallest part of a thing an entirety."[33]

Rodin's Reputation

From the time he first came to public notice with the display of *The Age of Bronze* at the 1877 Salon, Rodin's experimentation with sculptural conventions provoked vituperation from conservative critics and a corresponding level of adulation among those who responded to the sensuality and psychological drama achieved in his powerfully modeled forms. His more audacious accomplishments, including *The Burghers of Calais* and his proposed but rejected monuments to the writers Victor Hugo and Honoré de Balzac, provoked furious controversies. Yet his influence contributed to a major transformation in artistic understanding over the next four decades, as manifested, for example, by the omnipresence of the emotion-laden, fragmentary figure during the first decades of the new century. At the time of his death in 1917, Rodin was acknowledged as one of the fathers of European modernism. Following his death, his direct influence persisted for at least a generation. Even those sculptors who did not explicitly emulate his work had at least a Rodin "moment" as they explored the implications of his accomplishment in struggling to discover their personal sculptural language.

With the triumph of abstraction in the mid-twentieth century, Rodin's figure-centered work was reevaluated. His reputation—and his prices—sank as artists and critics saw his art not as the forerunner of modernism but as the most extreme expression of the academic tradition. During the final third of the century, however, the sculptor's critical fortunes revived in tandem with the resurgence of figurative art. Today Rodin is firmly ensconced within the canon of great sculptors. Scholars continue to probe the meanings of his compositions, and his works also continue to excite controversies, ranging from issues of censorship to questions regarding the concept of "originality" provoked by his working methods and by his will, which provides for the posthumous casting of his work. Because of their remarkable evocative power, Rodin's sculptures are as compelling for most viewers today as they were when the writer Arthur Symons first experienced them a century ago: "He endeavors to represent life in all its mystery, not to penetrate the mystery of life. He gives you a movement, an expression; if it has come straight from life, if it has kept the living contours, it must mean something, and he is but your comrade in the search for that meaning."[34]

Containing works in a variety of media, in differing scales, and from all phases of Rodin's career, the Cantor Arts Center collection mirrors in miniature the magnitude and variety of the sculptor's monumental achievement. It is hoped that the display of his works, accessible to all on the university campus, will excite continued critical inquiry as well as pleasure among our visitors.

Notes

1. For the sculptor's biography, see Ruth Butler, *Rodin: The Shape of Genius* (New Haven: Yale University Press, 1993); for a general survey of his life and work, see Robert Descharnes and J. E. Chabrun, *Auguste Rodin* (New York: Viking Press, 1967).

2. In 1875 Rodin sold the plaster as well as its reproduction rights to a Belgian foundry, Compagnie des Bronzes, for 750 francs (see Antoinette Le Normand-Romain, *Vers l'age d'airain: Rodin en Belgique*, exh. cat. [Paris: Musée Rodin, 1997], 150–52). That foundry continued to produce casts of *Suzon* into the 1930s.

3. Truman H. Bartlett, "Auguste Rodin, Sculptor," *American Architect and Building News* 25, no. 689 (1889), reprinted in *Auguste Rodin: Readings on His Life and Art*, ed. Albert Elsen (Englewood Cliffs, N.J.: Prentice-Hall, 1965), 21. Elsen reprinted Bartlett's series of ten articles published originally in the *American Architect and Building News* (1889).

4. Rodin's sculpture collection, comprising about sixty-four hundred works from the Near and Far East and from classical antiquity to about 1900, reflects his catholic tastes (see Bénédicte Garnier, *Rodin: Antiquity Is My Youth*, trans. K.-M. Bradford [Paris: Musée Rodin, 2002]). On Rodin's other collections, see Cécile Goldscheider, *Rodin collectionneur*, exh. cat. (Paris: Musée Rodin and Presses artistiques, 1967). For his correspondence, see Alain Beausire et al., eds., *Correspondence de Rodin*, 4 vols. (Paris: Musée Rodin, 1985–92); for his drawings, see Claudie Judrin, *Inventaire des dessins de Rodin*, 6 vols. (Paris: Musée Rodin, 1984–92). It is estimated that an additional three thousand drawings survive in public and private collections throughout the world (Claudie Judrin, *Rodin: Hell and Paradise: Sculptor's Drawings* [Paris: Musée Rodin, 2002], 5).

5. All the posthumous bronze casts are authentic and original insofar as they, like lifetime examples, were cast from the plasters and clay compositions modeled by Rodin. Even during his lifetime, the sculptor rarely involved himself in the production of the bronzes, which were cast more or less on demand for his international clientele. He preferred to leave such mechanical work to the craftsmen he employed and to the extraordinarily proficient employees of commercial foundries such as Leblanc-Barbedienne, Fumière et Gavignot, and Alexis Rudier. We rarely know the precise number of casts made during the sculptor's lifetime.

6. Bartlett, "Auguste Rodin, Sculptor," 107.

7. Gustave Geffroy, "The Sculptor Rodin" (1889), reprinted in Ruth Butler, ed., *Rodin in Perspective* (Englewood Cliffs, N.J.: Prentice-Hall, 1980), 64.

8. Bartlett, "Auguste Rodin, Sculptor," 107.

9. Camille Mauclair, "August Rodin, His Work, His Life, and His Influence" (1901) in Butler, ed., *Rodin in Perspective*, 110.

10. Bartlett, "Auguste Rodin, Sculptor," 107.

11. Mauclair, "Auguste Rodin," 110.

12. Anna de Noailles, cited in Frederic V. Grunfeld, *Rodin: A Biography* (New York: Henry Holt, 1987), 476.

13. Bartlett, "Auguste Rodin, Sculptor," 108.

14. According to Mauclair, "he has read very little and loves only a few books" ("Auguste Rodin," 110). On the contrary, the novelist Anatole France described Rodin as "a deeply learned artist and an ingenious innovator" ("The Gates of Hell," *Le Figaro*, 7 June 1900, reprinted in Butler, ed., Rodin in Perspective, 105).

15. See, for example, *Venus: To the Venus of Melos*, trans. Dorothy Dudley (New York: B. W. Huebsch, 1912); originally published as "Vénus: À la Vénus de Milo," *L'Art et les artistes* 10 (March 1910): 243–55; *Les Cathédrales de France* (Paris: Armand Colin, 1914); "La danse de Çiva," *Ars asiatica* 3 (1921): 9–13.

16. Rainer Maria Rilke, *Rodin*, trans. Jesse Lemont and Hans Trausil (New York: Fine Editions Press, 1945), reprinted in Elsen, ed., *Auguste Rodin*, 115.

17. See Alain Beausire, "Le Marcottage," in *La Sculpture française au XIXe siècle*, exh. cat. (Paris: Réunion des musées nationaux, 1986), 95–106.

18. Between 1898 and 1918, for example, at least 329 casts of *The Kiss* in four different sizes were made over the course of his twenty-year contract with the Leblanc-Barbedienne foundry (Antoinette Le Normand-Romain, *The Kiss*, trans. L. Davidson and Michael Gibson [Paris: Réunion des musées nationaux, 1995], 39–40).

19. Rilke, *Rodin*, in Elsen, ed., *Auguste Rodin*, 113.

20. On Rodin and photography, see Albert E. Elsen, *In Rodin's Studio* (Ithaca, N.Y.: Cornell University Press, 1980); Hélène Pinet, *Rodin sculpteur et les photographes de son temps* (Paris: P. Sers, 1985); and Hélène Pinet, "Montre est la question vitale: Rodin and Photography," in *Sculpture and Photography: Envisioning the Third Dimension*, ed. G. A. Johnson (Cambridge: Cambridge University Press, 1998), 68–85. The Cantor Arts Center collection includes 110 examples: see Albert E. Elsen with Rosalyn Frankel Jamison, *Rodin's Art: The Rodin Collection of the Iris and B. Gerald Cantor Center for Visual Arts at Stanford University*, ed. Bernard Barryte (New York: Oxford University Press, 2003), cat. A58–A87 (photographs of Rodin), cat. A90–A171 (photographs of Rodin's works).

21. Antoinette Le Normand-Romain, *Rodin en 1900: L'exposition de l'Alma*, exh. cat. (Paris: Réunion des musées nationaux, 2001), 274–341. See also *Eugene Druet, 1868–1916*, exh. cat. (New York: Sander Gallery, 1993).

22. Claire Black, "Edward Steichen's *Rodin—Le Penseur*: The Rhetoric of a Photograph," *Cantor Arts Center Journal* 2 (2000–2001): 32–47.

23. Elsen, *Rodin's Art*, cat. 49.

24. Ibid., cat. 20.

25. Albert E. Elsen, "Rodin's 'Perfect Collaborator': Henri Lebossé," in *Rodin Rediscovered*, ed. Albert E. Elsen, exh. cat. (Washington, D.C.: National Gallery of Art, 1981), 249–59.

26. Elsen, *Rodin's Art*, cat. 64, 65.

27. Nicole Barbier, "Assemblages de Rodin," in *Le Corps en morceaux*, exh. cat. (Paris: Réunion des musées nationaux, 1990), 241–46.

28. Bartlett, "Auguste Rodin, Sculptor," 163.

29. Henri-Charles-Etienne Dujardin-Beaumetz, "Rodin's Reflections on Art," in Elsen, ed., *Auguste Rodin*, 167–68.

30. Rodolphe Darzens, "A Visit to Rodin's Studio," *La Jeune France* (January 1888), in Butler, ed., *Rodin in Perspective*, 56.

31. Judith Cladel, *Rodin: L'Oeuvre et l'homme* (Brussels: Van Oest, 1908), 97.

32. Michel Georges-Michel, *Peintres et sculpteurs que j'ai connu, 1900–1942* (New York: Brentano's, 1942), 264.

33. Rilke, *Rodin*, in Elsen, ed., *Auguste Rodin*, 123

34. Arthur Symons, "Rodin," *Fortnightly Review*, June 1902, 963, in Butler, ed., *Rodin in Perspective*, 117.

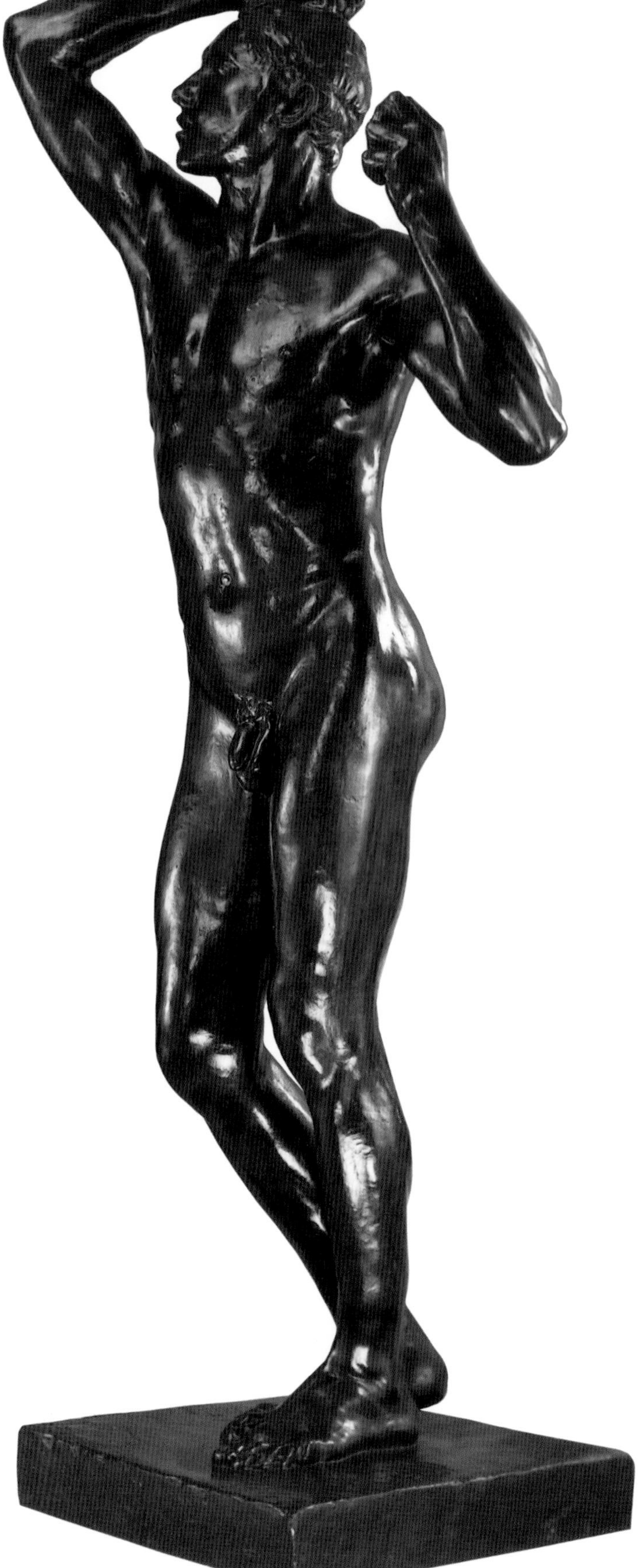

Highlights

OF THE COLLECTION

The Age of Bronze
1876

Anchoring the collection of the Cantor Arts Center is Rodin's first public statue (fig. 42), represented by a cast dated about 1920, just after the sculptor's death.[1] The statue's original title, *The Vanquished*, reflects its origin as a tribute to the heroism of French soldiers who displayed valor even though their nation suffered defeat in the Franco-Prussian War of 1870.

Doing journeyman work in Belgium at the age of thirty-seven, Rodin longed to establish his reputation as an independent sculptor rather than to spend the rest of his life as an artisan working for others. With this statue he presented his personal system of modeling the human form not just from the front, sides, and back, but continuously, so that fluent, articulated profiles rewarded the viewer who moves fully around the statue. He thus democratized the body by showing that in a well-made sculpture from life, all views—not just the front—were expressive.

Just before the life-size statue's initial showing, Rodin removed the spear that had been held in the youth's outstretched left hand. Although this may have been done to encourage uninterrupted study of all the profiles, it had other important implications. Removal of the attribute diminished specificity of meaning; renaming the sculpture similarly served to liberate the evocative potential of the figure. An artist who considered the human body

42
[OPPOSITE]
The Age of Bronze, 1875–76
Alexis Rudier foundry, c. 1920
180.4 × 50.8 × 50.8
1983.300 (cat. 1)

as a wholly sufficient and inexhaustible bearer of meaning, Rodin must have intended these consequences. Attributes are rare in his subsequent works, and names given to individual figures and to groups—names that frequently changed over time—generally served to expand rather than to restrict the possible range of interpretations.

Described on its debut as everything from "a curious *atelier* study with a very pretentious name" to a "mysterious personage . . . molded out of suffering and dreams,"[2] *The Age of Bronze* was especially admired by young artists for bringing sculpture closer to life. It was faulted by several critics, however, for ambiguity of meaning, for not correcting the physical deficiencies of the model, and even for being cast from life. This last was a libel on Rodin's method and integrity. Deeply hurt, he managed to vindicate himself. Edmond Turquet, a fair-minded undersecretary of state for fine arts, recognized the injustice, and with faith in the little-known but controversial middle-aged sculptor, he gave Rodin the commission for *The Gates of Hell*.

The Gates of Hell
(1880–1900) AND ITS PROGENY

In 1880 Turquet commissioned the forty-year-old Rodin to make a bronze door (fig. 43) for a new museum of decorative arts. Awarding the commission to the relatively unknown sculptor was a daring act for a government official, but the undersecretary of state for fine arts had been among those who supported Rodin against accusations that *The Age of Bronze* had been cast from life. As the figures on the commissioned door would be smaller than life size and in relief, Rodin was convinced that he would win public vindication for his method of modeling. Unusually, the sculptor rather than the patron proposed the subject: sculptures in relief based on Dante's *Divine Comedy*. This epic had preoccupied Rodin for many years, and it was a subject with which the public was familiar and that other French sculptors of the early Third Republic—for example, Jean-Baptiste Carpeaux—had occasionally interpreted in statuary shown in the great public Salons. Because the commission specified neither the portal's size (probably because the museum had not yet been designed and, in fact, was never built) nor its content, the sculptor was, uniquely, left to his own devices. Rodin may never have known for sure if his sculpture was to serve as a symbolic portal or actually be used, whether it would be outside or inside the museum, or if it

43
[OPPOSITE]
The Gates of Hell, 1880–c. 1900
Cast 1981, no. 5
639.8 × 401.3 × 84.8
1985.86 (cat. 37)

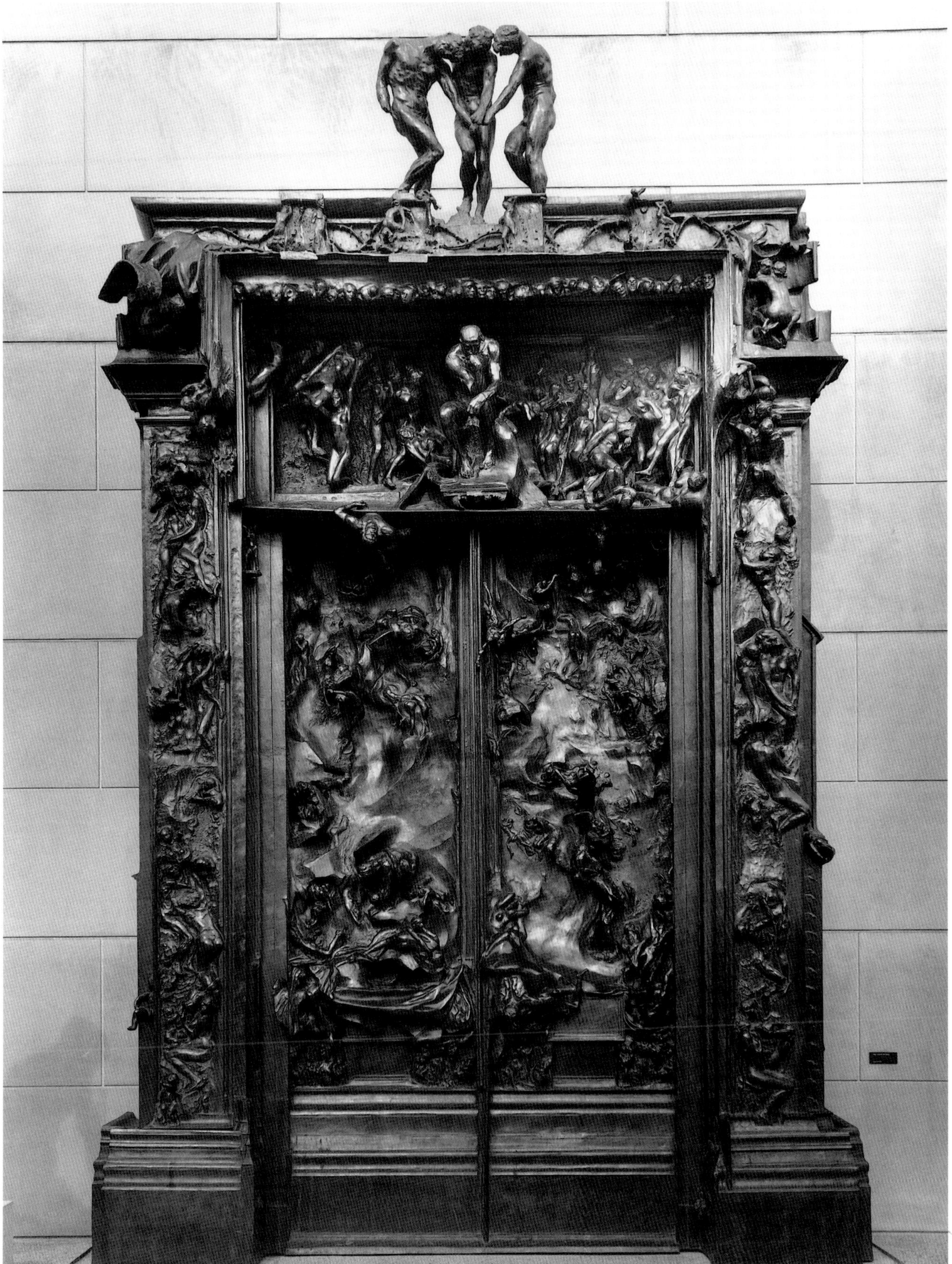

did function, whether it would open out or in. Preliminary architectural sketches show that he conceived of a series of rectangular panels in low relief to be set into the portal following the precedent of Lorenzo Ghiberti's famous *Gates of Paradise* (1425–52) for the Baptistery in Florence.

At least since 1875, Rodin's readings in Dante had inspired him to make freely interpretive drawings based on certain episodes in the *Inferno*. By 1877 he had made a life-size sculpture of a seated Ugolino. There is no evidence that he ever seriously contemplated modeling episodes from Dante's *Purgatory* or *Paradise*. Rodin's interpretive or "black" drawings, so named for their mood as well as their dark tonality, appear for the most part untranslatable into sculpture.[3] At the time of the commission, he was obviously relying upon his imagination and limited experience with narrative reliefs to carry out what would have been a traditional storied portal. It was when he actually began to create a study for the portal in clay and also to work from living models in his studio that he broke with the tradition of the relief-panel format and its distinct episodic divisions (fig. 44).

By the end of the first year of work, Rodin, who had no previous experience with a monumental composition, made a momentous decision and took a staggering gamble by forgoing the explicit illustration of Dante's *Inferno* and abandoning the idea of a preplanned composition. For what must have seemed to be the most important project of his career, the sculptor decided to work from life rather than literature and *improvise* the composition on an epic scale. He had gone so far as to make a few sculptures based on Dante but decided to let his modeling of living men and women evoke the general tone of the portal's drama. Truman Bartlett reports Rodin as saying of the *Gates*: "My sole idea is simply one of color and effect. There is no intention of classification or method of subject, no scheme of illustration or intended moral purpose. I followed my imagination, my own sense of arrangement, movement, and composition." The result, Bartlett concluded, "represents a perpendicular section of the damned world."[4]

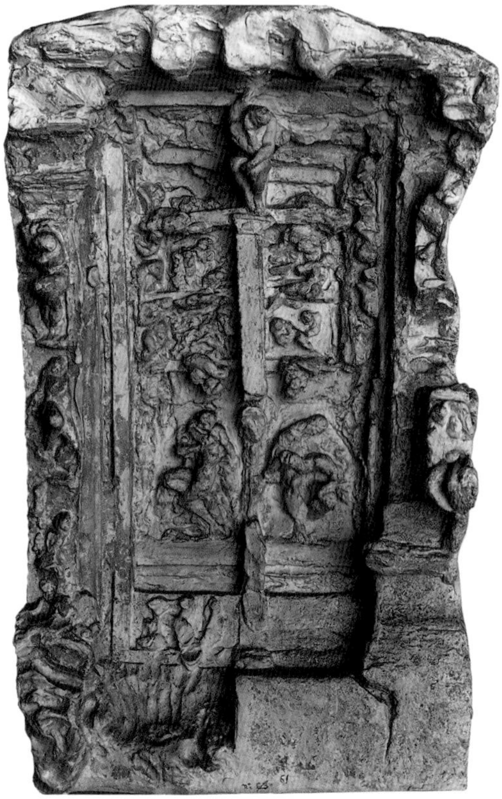

44
Third Model for "The Gates of Hell," 1880
Plaster
111.5 × 75 × 30
Collection Musée Rodin, Paris

The Gates of Hell, as Rodin's portal came to be called before 1900, may have begun as the illustration of a medieval literary epic, but it ended as the artist's personal vision incorporating themes gleaned particularly from the writings of Victor Hugo and Charles Baudelaire. It is thus a poetic rather than a theological inferno. Between statues of Adam and Eve portrayed after the Fall, Rodin improvised an epic tragedy of men, women, and children who, without exception and through all time, are hopelessly victims of the passions that cause their ceaseless movement. Hell is chaos. It is unconfined, and just as sculpture and frame intermingle, there is no hierarchy of suffering within the asymmetry of the portal. Rodin had for all intents and purposes stopped work on his portal after 1900, but long before that time the turbulent surface had become an expression of the sculptor's view of humanity's incapacity to find spiritual peace or achieve the fulfillment of its hopes. In the lower inside right corner of the portal, where we expect a signature, Rodin modeled in low relief a possible self-portrait as a naked, bearded man in profile, his legs drawn up under him, his left hand against his forehead and his right hand holding the small splayed form of a woman.

Using a government-owned studio, Rodin worked on this commission for more than twenty years. Since he was never pressed to deliver it and because he had to support himself, he worked on many other projects concurrently. He created the *Gates* as he did other compositions, modeling his sculptures in clay, piece by piece, and then casting them in plaster. He would test the works by mounting them on a large wooden armature, which in time was replaced by a plaster framework. Figures in high relief or in the round would be subsequently removed and numbered for reinstallation in order to avoid breakage as he and his assistants worked on scaffolding before the portal. By 1900 he had enlarged the height of the door from its original twelve feet to its present twenty feet, to which were added the three figures atop the portal, known as *The Three Shades*. Presiding over the sealed entrance is a single, stationary figure. Massive and silent, *The Thinker* was conceived in 1880 for the *Gates* (fig. 45). He is the contemplative artist who gives society an image of itself in aesthetic form: the *Gates* are the vision, and *The Thinker* the visionary. Although the artist experiences life, Rodin made *The Thinker* blind (without irises in his eyes) and mute (sealing the mouth with his hand) in order to show that during the moments of creation sensory distraction must be ignored in order to concentrate on an inner vision. *The Thinker*'s powerful body foretells the labor demanded by artistic creation in the wake of thought; his location pays tribute to the intellectual and spiritual centrality of the artist in society.

Rodin planned the first one-sculptor retrospective in history to take place in 1900, during the great Paris World's Fair, but when he revealed his *Gates* to the public in June, not all the figures had been reinstalled, perhaps for lack of time. Critical reception of the denuded portal was mixed. The

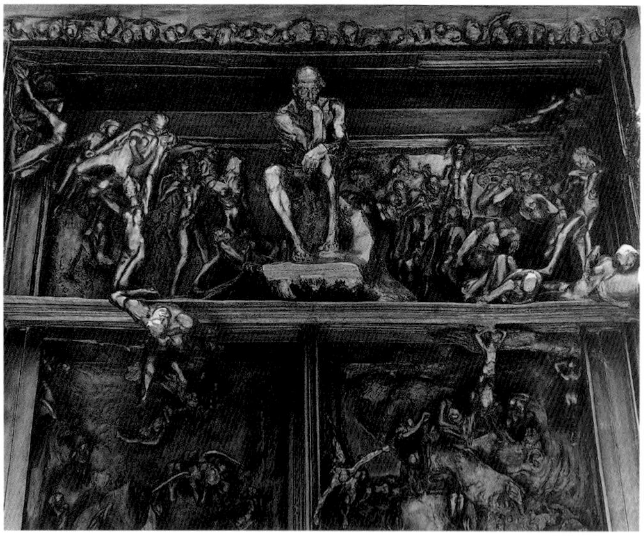

government made no official move to have the work cast for the museum, and so Rodin kept the plaster portal and its numerous detached parts in his studios. To date, seven casts have been made of the *Gates*, and all are posthumous. The first two bronze examples were not cast until 1928. The cast commissioned by B. Gerald Cantor and donated to Stanford University was the fifth, and the first made using the lost-wax process, as specified by Rodin.[5]

When Rodin explained that his portal had started as "Dante's Hell," he could refer to certain figures and groups that dated from its earliest phase, when he was interpreting the *Inferno*. These are *Ugolino and His Sons* (fig. 46); *Paolo and Francesca*, just below Ugolino (fig. 47); and *The Three Shades* (fig. 48), atop the door. Some scholars argue that Rodin originally intended *The Thinker* to be Dante, but although Rodin did not discourage this identification, the muscular figure who surveys the writhing multitudes cannot be directly equated with the "thin ascetic," as the sculptor referred to the poet. Rather, *The Thinker* is more directly inspired by the writings of Baudelaire and

45
[ABOVE]
Detail of *The Gates of Hell*: tympanum with *The Thinker*

46
[BELOW RIGHT]
Ugolino and His Sons, 1881–82
Plaster
41 × 63.5 × 40.5
1987.38 (cat. 45)

47
[OPPOSITE TOP]
Paolo and Francesca, 1881–84
Cast 1973, 2/12
31.8 × 57.8 × 41.9
1998.361 (cat. 50)

48
[OPPOSITE BOTTOM]
The Three Shades, 1881–83
Cast 1978, 8/12
97.8 × 90.2 × 45.1
1998.360 (cat. 43)

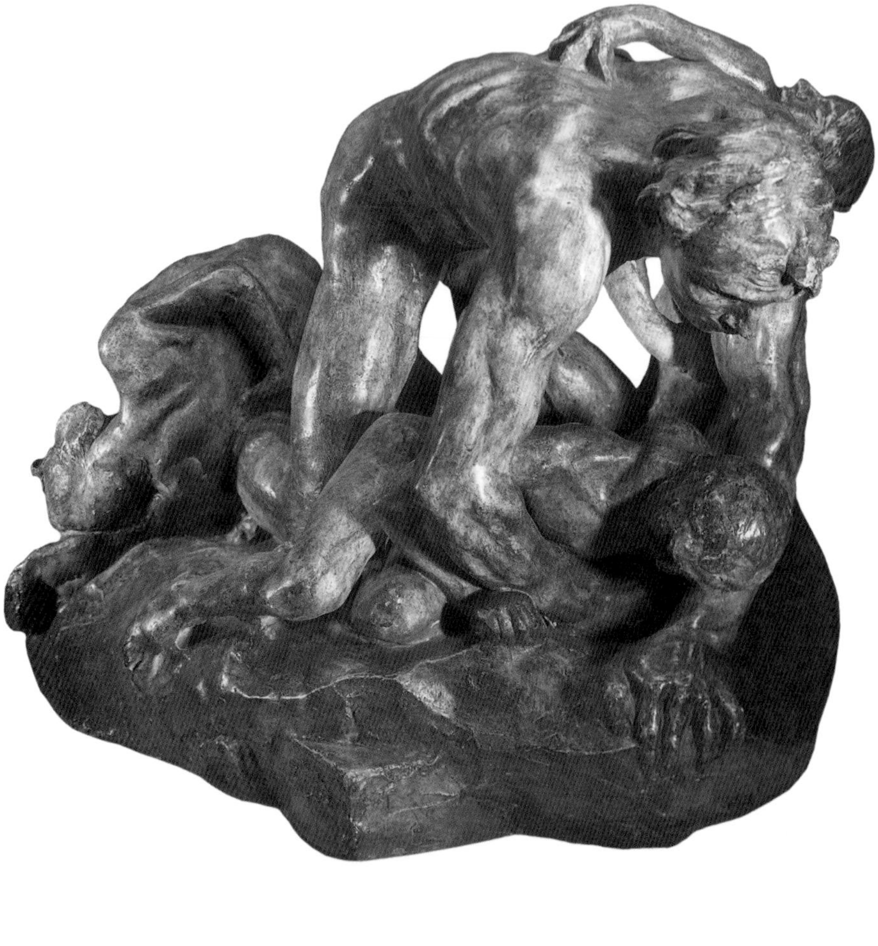

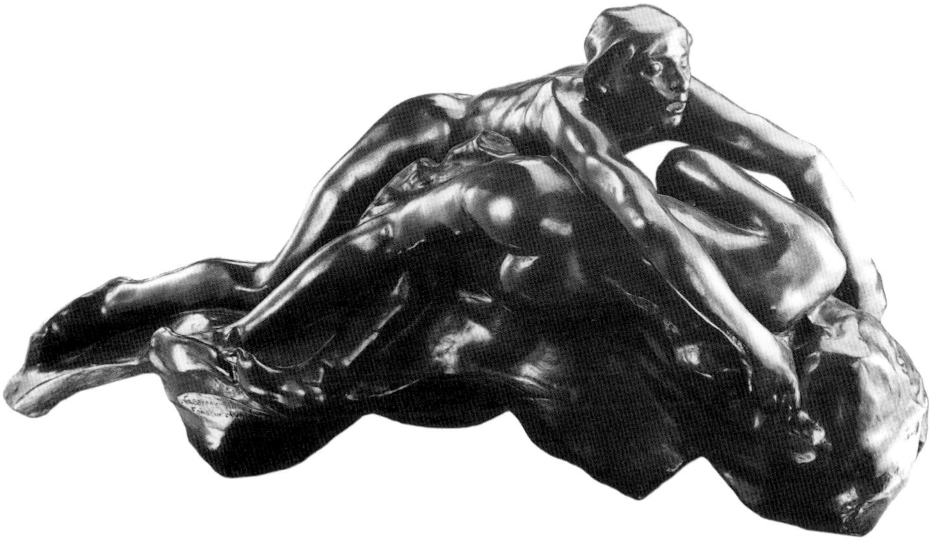

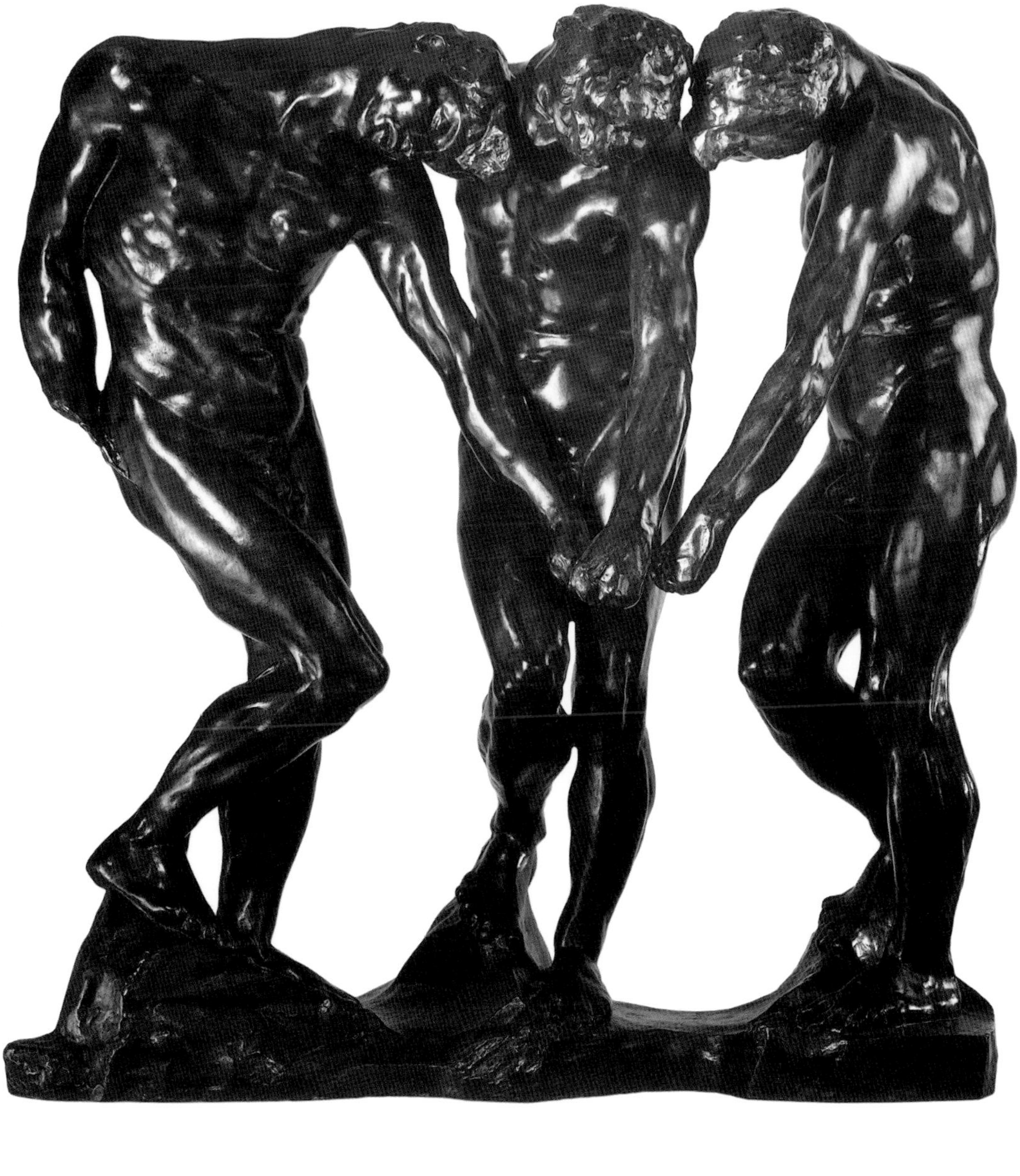

Hugo, representing the poet-artist who thoughtfully re-creates his society, gives tangible aesthetic form to its hopes and fears, and reveals humanity to itself through art. Remaining as well is the spirit of Dante's narrative, specifically the uncertain geography that is traversed and the way in which figures emerge from an amorphous realm to engage the narrator with the story that explains their plight before again sinking into the mass of tormented souls.

What do we make of the anguished, despairing population of Rodin's dismal bronze world? More than a place, hell for Rodin was a state of mind. For him, men and women carry the means of their eternal torment within themselves in the form of insatiable passions. For Baudelaire and other nineteenth-century writers and artists, church and state no longer offered credible and stabilizing alternatives to the human condition—to what Rilke called the "invisible conflicts" of the age[6]—and Rodin shared their pessimistic view of man's fate. Hell beyond the tomb continued earthly torment. When Rodin mingled fallen angels and centaurs with nameless men, women, and children, he was synthesizing past and present, as if to tell us that life was ever so. Hell for Rodin was to be thrown back upon the self. His crowds are of individuals, intertwined but not mutually communicative. Their fate is perpetual striving, the will to act without the hope of success: children are held, for example, but ineffectually comforted. To call all of these figures sinners is to assume that Rodin was moralizing, a stance he rejected. The artist in the person of *The Thinker* has replaced Christ in the seat of judgment, but he does not condemn from a book of laws. He is a compassionate observer, although he is blind, and if he is a judge, he is also a prisoner of the realm he surveys. In the additive process of composing the *Gates*, Rodin had rejected not only conventional narrative but also medieval and Renaissance devices for order because they symbolized theological views he did not hold. For example, the traditional symbolism of right and left, high and low, which he may have adopted from Catholic depictions of the Last Judgment, are absent, for this symbolic language has no applicability in Rodin's seething geography, where there are no sinners and no salvation.

Rodin unquestionably wanted a modern alternative not only to the great medieval Last Judgments but also to that of Michelangelo in the Sistine Chapel (fig. 49). Rodin's achievement was to give imaginative coherence to a theme of spiritual chaos. To recognize how he accomplished this, one must step back from the portal and its sea of movement and take in the composition as a whole. Only then does one see how the various sections have been

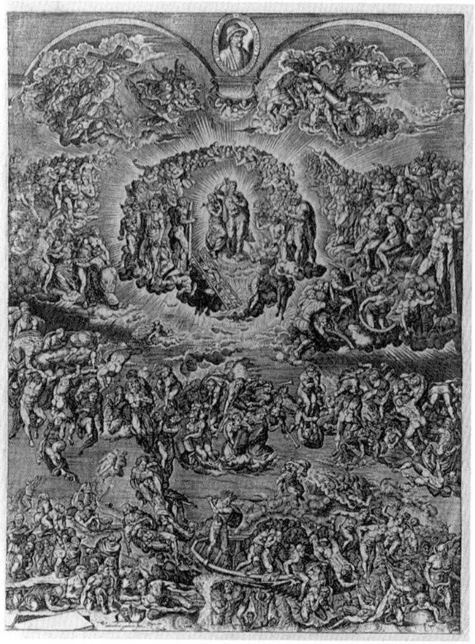

49
Léonard Gaultier
(c. 1552–1641)
Last Judgment (after Michelangelo)
Etching and engraving
(LeBlanc 18)
30.8 × 22.9
Robert M. Loeser Collection, 1944.2.70

visually weighted and how the figural clusters and empty spaces achieve an asymmetrical, three-dimensional balance that also harmonizes with the rectilinear frame. Not only did Rodin model in all degrees of relief, but he also designed an architectural surround that helped to stabilize the heaving sculptural forms while also responding to the figures that press against, overlap, or cling to the framing borders, eliding the distinction between sculpture and architecture. As Rodin put it, "In decorative sculpture, beautiful composition comes from . . . the balance of the relationship of movements and by the proportion of the sculptured part with the architectural support."[7] What makes this sculptor's achievement particularly audacious is the monumental scale on which he achieved this unprecedented decorative unity.

Just a few years after he began work on *The Gates of Hell*, Rodin started to exhibit and sell as independent sculptures figures and groups made for the portal, whether or not they were to be part of the final work. This practice allowed him to earn money to support himself, since the government was paying only his expenses for this costly project. It also made critics, artists, and the public aware of the portal's extraordinary artistic promise and Rodin's growth and range as a sculptor. It was the artist's hope to have the government pay for life-size statues of *Adam* and *Eve* (figs. 50, 51), which he intended to flank the portal, but this proposal was rejected. Nevertheless, Rodin exhibited these figures and modified the *Adam* and tripled its form to produce the half-life-size trio called *The Three Shades* atop the great door, which were themselves subsequently cast in different sizes (see fig. 48).

The *Gates* served Rodin as a thematic quarry through much of his career. Early on, he removed *The Kiss* from the *Gates* because he felt that it was too self-sufficient. This early rendition of Paolo and Francesca was exhibited as an independent composition, and the government paid to have it carved in marble. This version was shown simultaneously with Rodin's project for a monument to Balzac in 1898 (see fig. 67). By contrast with the negative reception given to the Balzac monument (which was rejected by the committee that had commissioned it), the paired lovers were a great public success, although many were disturbed by their nudity and preferred them as conventionally portrayed in period costume. From his second version of *Paolo and Francesca* (see fig. 47), Rodin enlarged the head of Francesca, and it became known as the *Head of Sorrow* (fig. 52), uttering a cry of anguish that epitomized the despair of all in *The Gates of Hell*. How often a work was exhibited and how Rodin manipulated the motif by enlargement, subtraction,

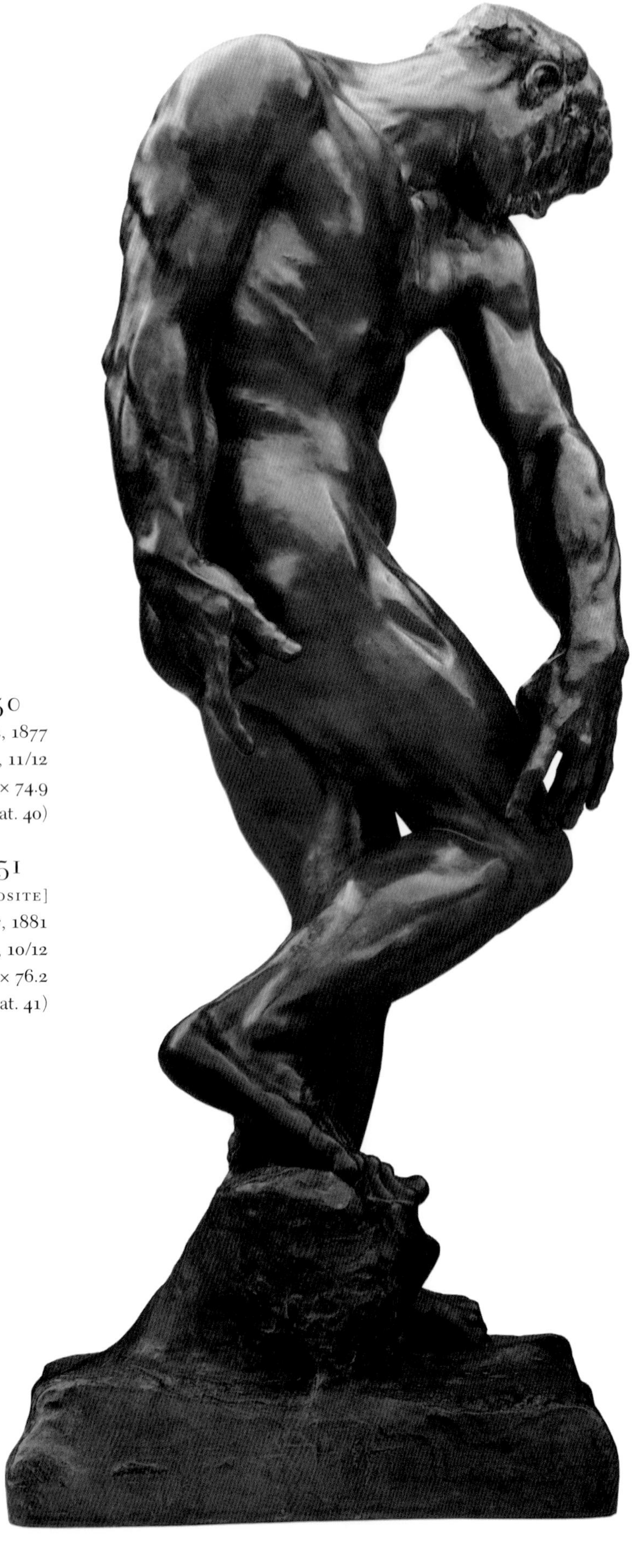

50
Adam, 1877
Cast 1974, 11/12
191.8 × 74.9 × 74.9
1985.15 (cat. 40)

51
[OPPOSITE]
Eve, 1881
Cast 1970, 10/12
172.2 × 60.3 × 76.2
1992.151 (cat. 41)

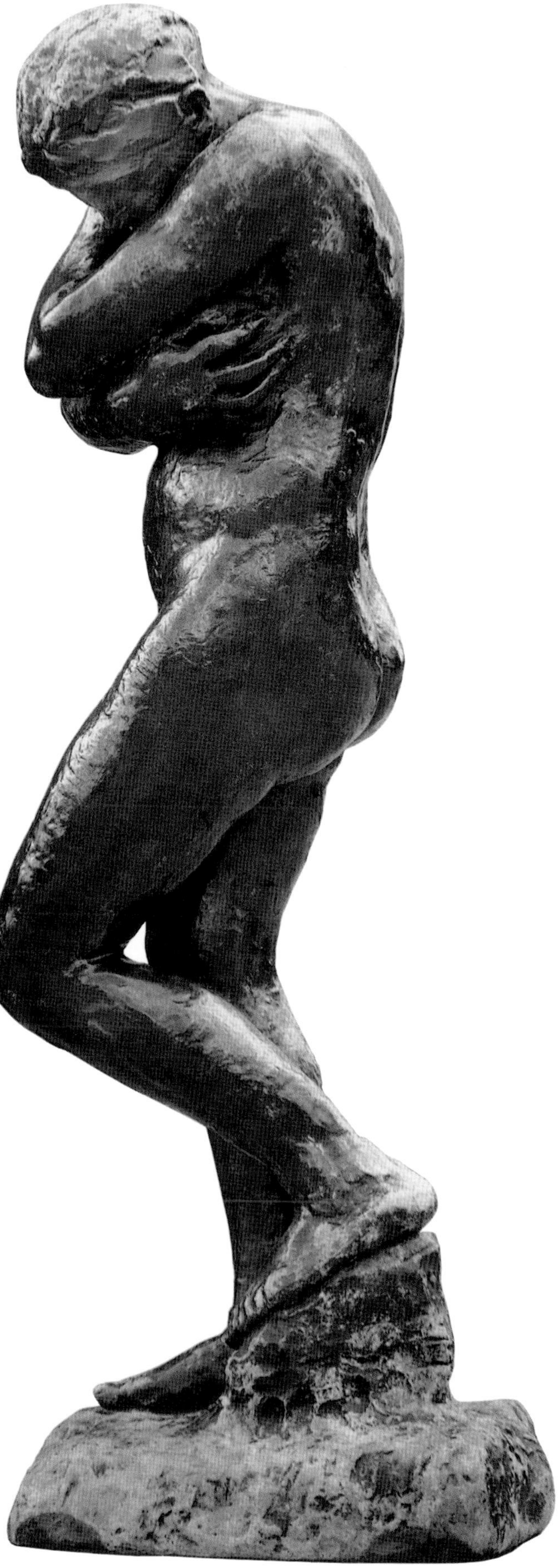

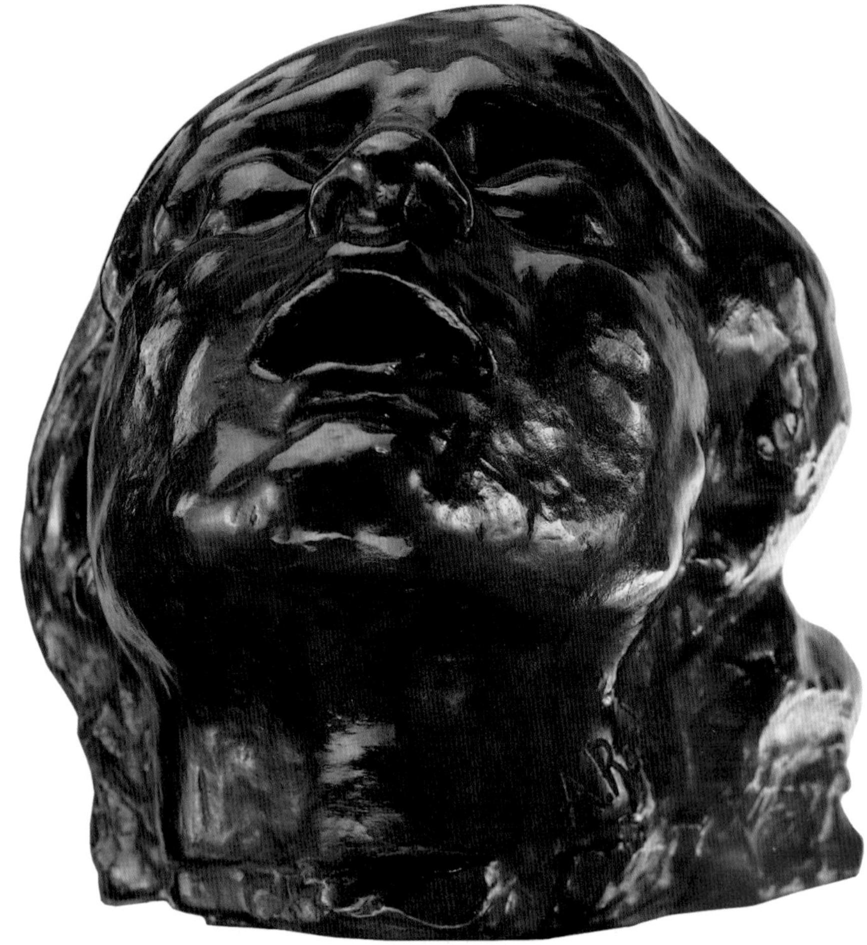

52
Head of Sorrow, 1882
Cast 1963, 11/12
24 × 21.6 × 20.3
1974.78 (cat. 55)

multiplication, and coupling with another figure indicated how much he cared for a particular pose or composition. Enlarged to life size and repositioned, for example, *The Martyr* (fig. 53) is derived from the figure of Francesca; likewise the torso and head were reutilized in *Meditation with Arms* and *Meditation without Arms* (figs. 54, 55).[8]

The two casts of *Meditation* are derived from a one-third-life-size figure in the extreme right corner of the lintel to the right of *The Thinker*. Possibly posed for by Rodin's mistress the sculptor Camille Claudel, this was one of the artist's favorite sculptures. As was his custom, he first made the woman's torso, the expressive nucleus and pivotal area for all his figures, to which he then added the head and legs (for which Claudel did not model). Without

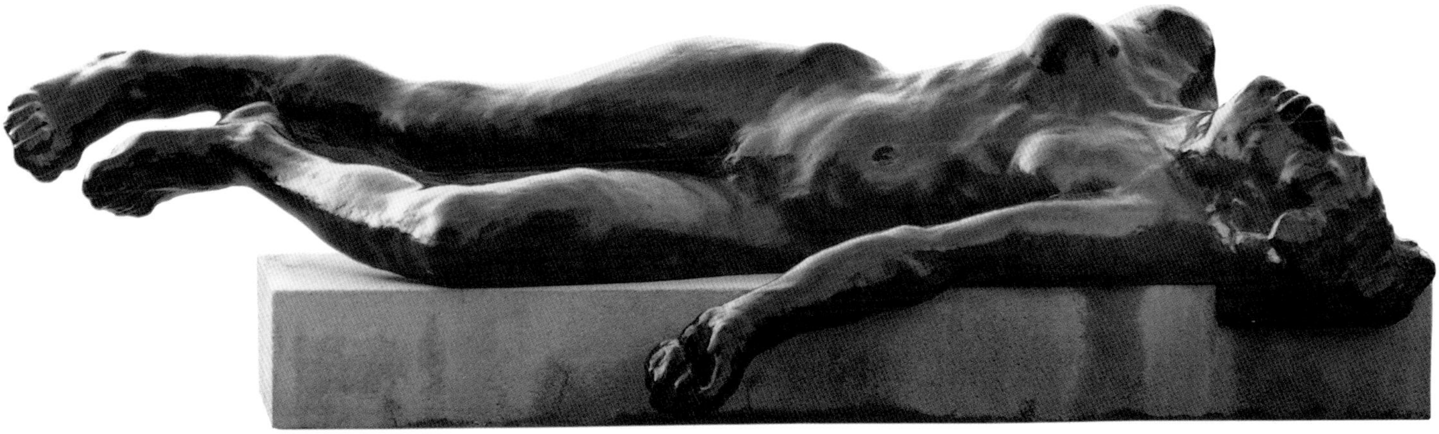

adjusting the shoulders (as one can see from the back), he rudely added sets of arms in different positions. The version without arms and a kneecap is not a study but a work finished by subtraction, opening the upper area of the body to the light and tightening the lower silhouette. When asked about its "incomplete" state, Rodin exclaimed: "Believe me, I left my statue in this condition on purpose. My figure represents *meditation*. This is why she has no arms for taking action, nor legs for walking. Haven't you noticed that when reflection is carried very far it suggests such plausible arguments for the most opposite decisions that in effect it recommends inertia?"[9] Commingling illusion and artifice, the exposed casting seams on the torso augment the sense of movement, and like the lines on a topographical map, allow us to see the nuanced modeling of the curved surface. Moreover, these seeming anomalies are functional. The roughened surfaces and casting seams remaining on this figure are deliberate artistic decisions that allow the sculpture to hold the surface plane under brilliant sunlight, to not flatten out or seem to dissolve. Rodin transformed what in his day was known as an étude, or study, into a complete work of art. The intimacy, freedom, and spontaneity associated with studies made in and for the privacy of the studio, which are usually lost in traditionally "finished" public sculptures, were what Rodin wanted to preserve even in large-scale public art. Rather than the beginnings of sculptures, these are conclusions arrived at by subtracting all that was unnecessary to clothe an expressive and beautiful movement. Irrelevant heads, arms, and legs were no more immune from subtraction than literary titles, identifying props, historical costumes, or any drapery whatsoever.

53
The Martyr, 1885,
enlarged 1899–1900
Cast 1983, 8/8
152.4 × 105.4 × 35.6
1998.351 (cat. 73)

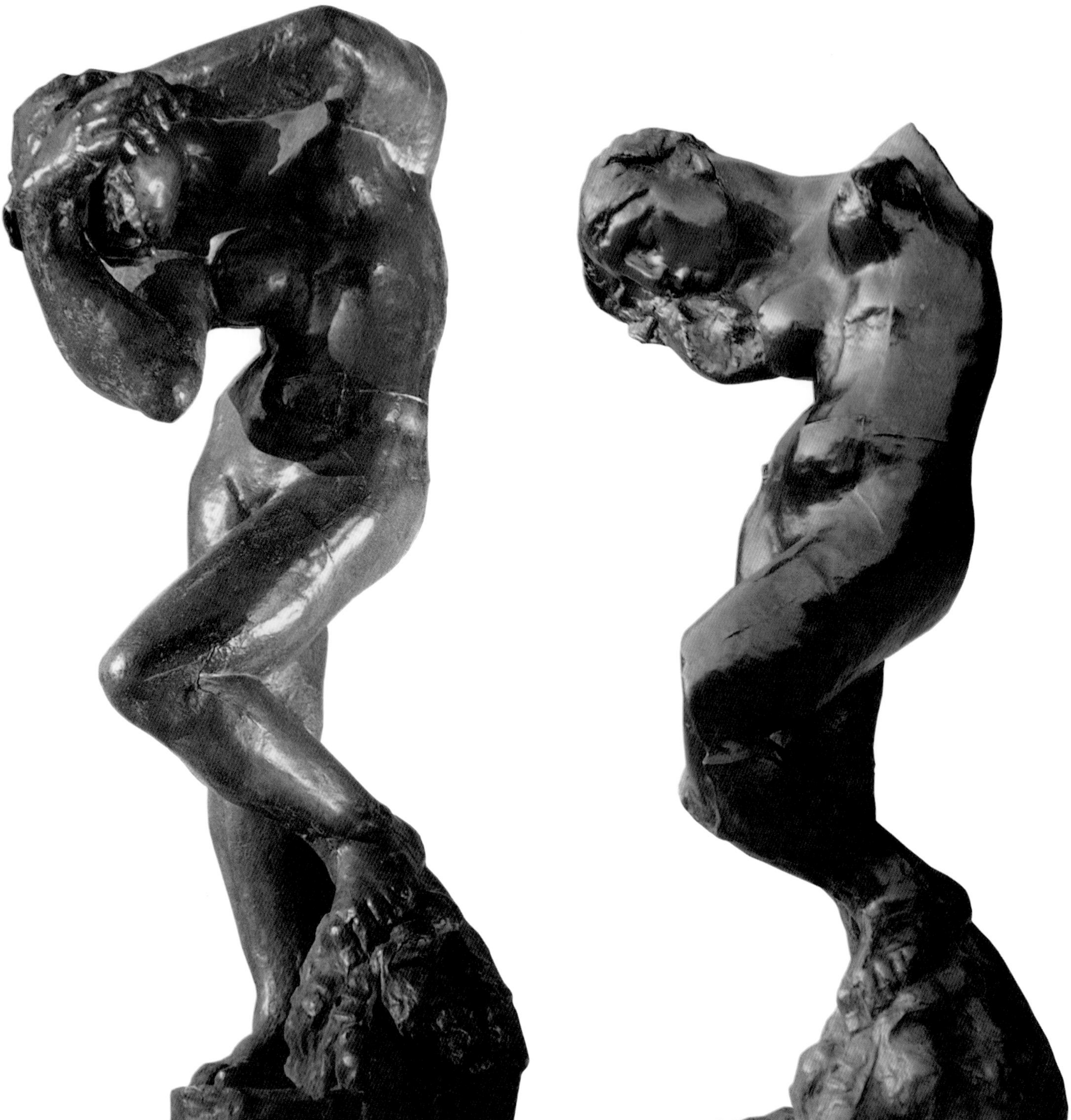

Although the commission for the *Gates* specified reliefs, Rodin's method of making a relief entailed first making a figure in the round. He would then cut away what he did not need when the form was applied to a surface, while he kept plasters of the whole figure intact. By this means he could introduce figures in all levels of relief (including freestanding figures) into a monumental composition destined to be the entrance to a museum of decorative arts. Making forms in the round, such as the lesbian couple titled *The Metamorphoses of Ovid* (fig. 56), allowed Rodin to vary their orientation within the *Gates* from that emphasized when he showed the motif separately. Often, as with *The Falling Man* (see fig. 28), located high up on the portal, clinging to the tympanum just below the feet of *The Thinker*, it is only when a form has been detached from the portal that we can experience its full expressiveness. *A Damned Woman* (fig. 57), to give another example, lies on her back in the right corner of the tympanum and cannot really be seen from the ground. When Rodin reused figures, he typically made no anatomical adjustment for the body's changed position in relation to gravity. Having in the collection so many sculptures derived from *The Gates of Hell* helps us to understand why Rodin referred to this heroic project as his "Noah's Ark."

54
[OPPOSITE LEFT]
Meditation with Arms, after 1900
Cast 1979, 7/12
156 × 74 × 66
1984.429 (cat. 62)

55
[OPPOSITE RIGHT]
Meditation without Arms, c. 1894, enlarged 1895–96
Cast 1981, 2/8
146 × 76.2 × 55.9
1992.136 (cat. 61)

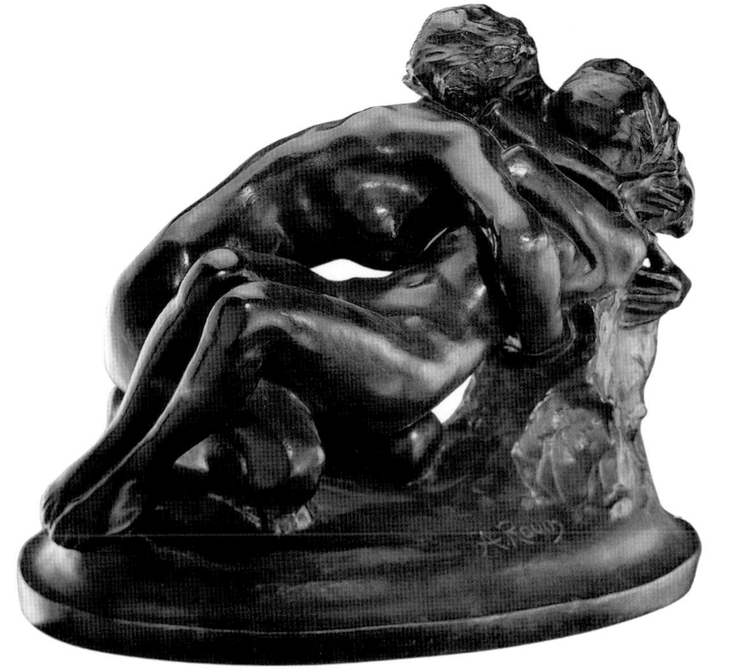

56
[BELOW LEFT]
The Metamorphoses of Ovid, c. 1884
Cast 1972, 6/12
33 × 40 × 26
1974.42 (cat. 68)

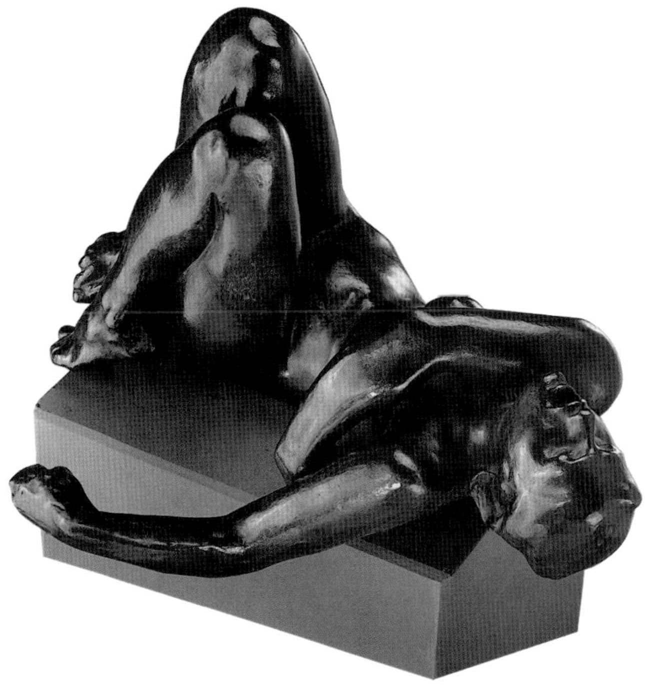

57
[BELOW]
Study for "A Damned Woman," c. 1884
Cast 1966, 10/12
20.3 × 39.5 × 26
1974.61 (cat. 63)

58
The Burghers of Calais in Memorial Court, Stanford University

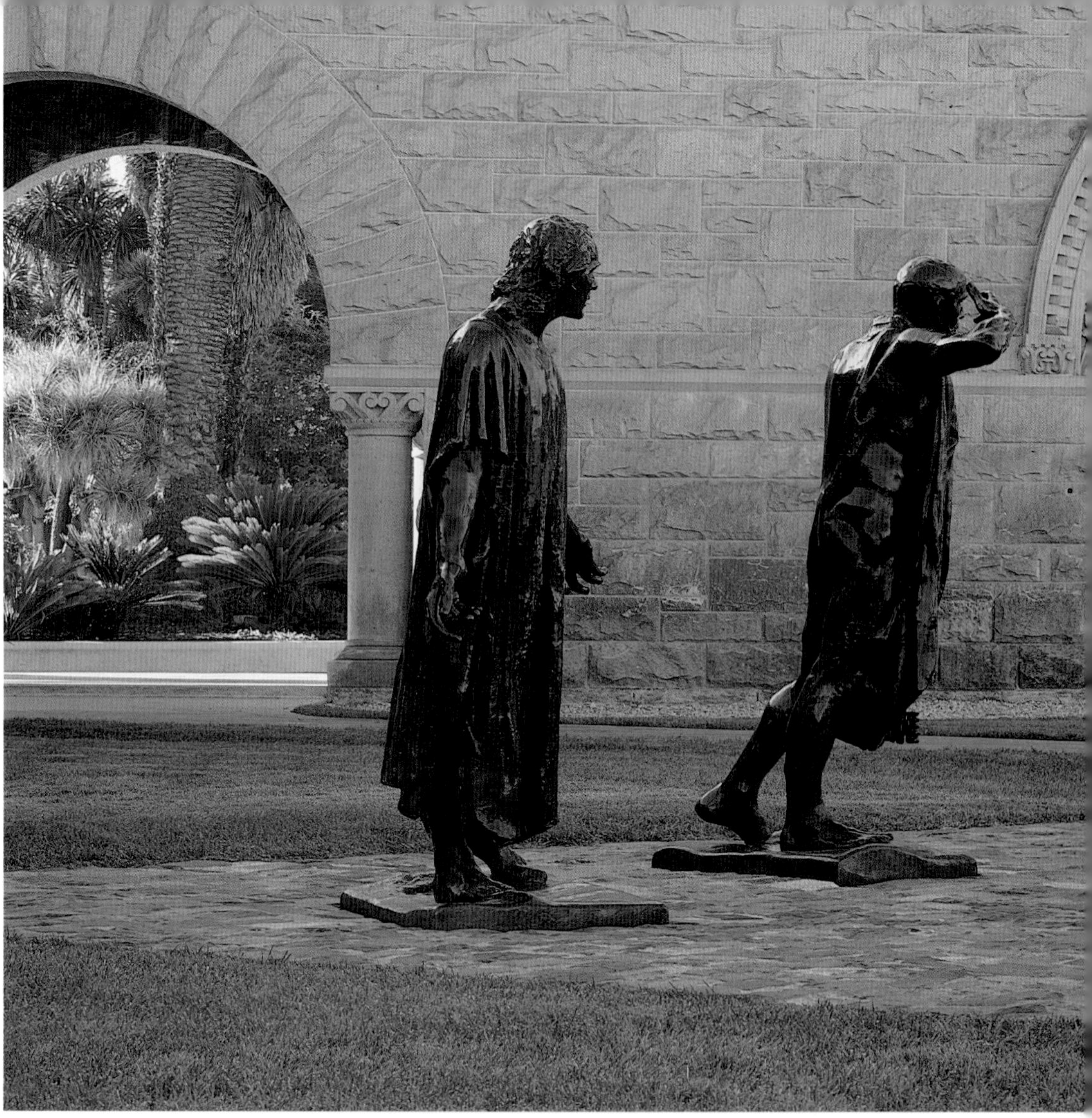

The Burghers of Calais

HEROISM IN DEFEAT

Rodin drew the subject for his *Burghers of Calais* (fig. 58) from Jean Froissart's medieval account of the siege of Calais in the fourteenth century by Edward, king of England. The French king saw this fortress city as crucial to protecting the borders of his kingdom but was unable to relieve it. The prolonged siege was bitterly fought, and the English suffered serious losses among their best knights. When the starving citizens of Calais parlayed for a surrender, King Edward demanded that they put themselves at his mercy, with no guarantee that their lives would be spared. The English barons objected that this was a terrible precedent in future wars between the two countries, and the king relented, saying:

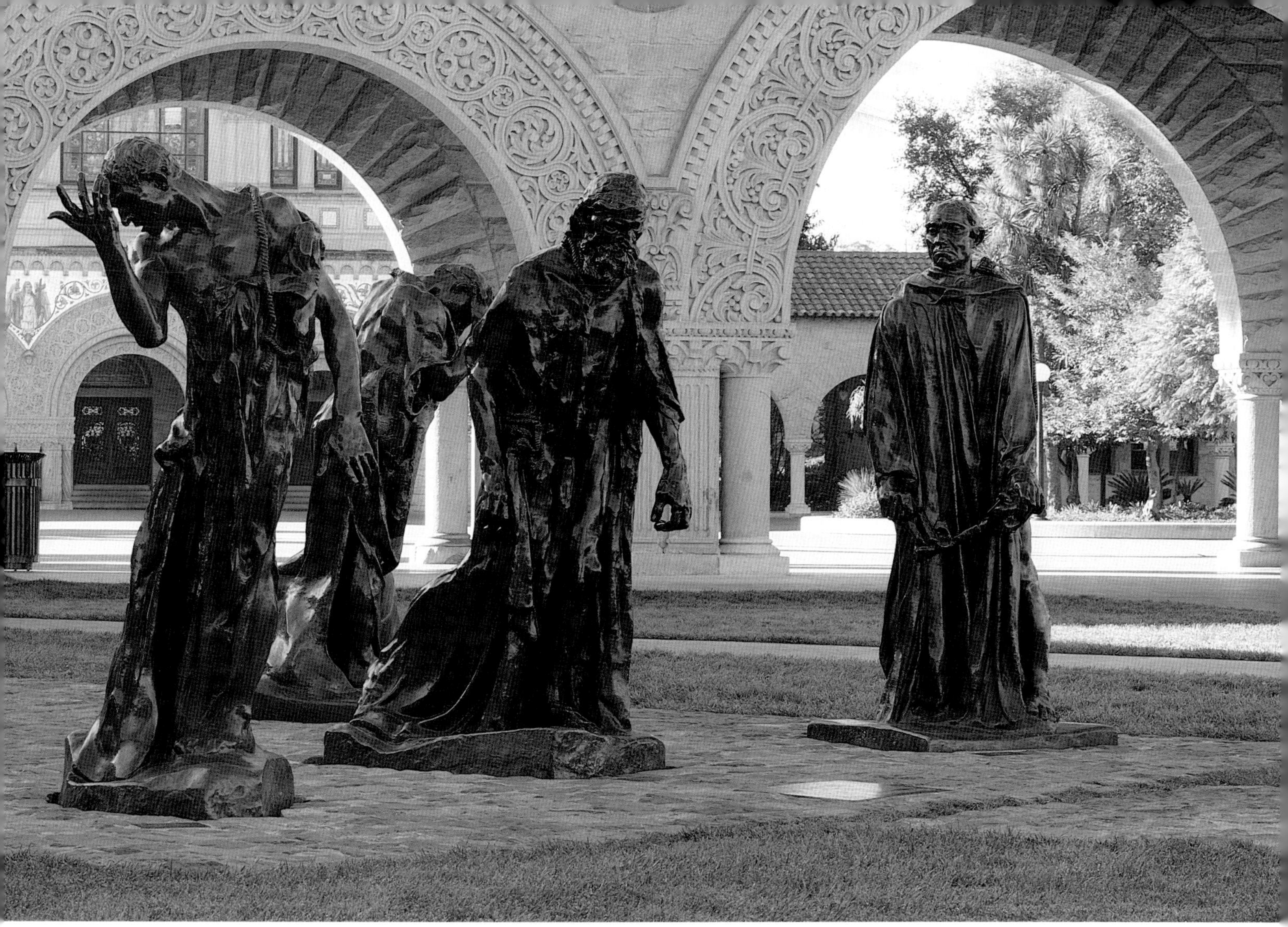

"My lords, I do not want to be alone against you all. . . . Go back to Calais and tell its commander that this is the limit of my clemency: six of the principal citizens are to come out, with their heads and their feet bare, halters round their necks and the keys of the town and castle in their hands. With these six I shall do as I please, and the rest I will spare."

Jean de Vienne was told Edward's decision and assembled the people, who came "though they were so weak with hunger that they could scarcely stand." He

repeated all that had been said, telling them that nothing more could be hoped for and asking them to consult together and give their answer quickly. When he had finished speaking they began to cry out and weep. At last the richest citizen of the town, by name Master Eustache de Saint-Pierre, stood up and

> said: "Sirs, it would be a cruel and miserable thing to allow such a population as this to die, so long as some remedy can be found. To prevent such a misfortune would surely be an act of great merit in Our Savior's eyes and, for my part, I should have such strong hopes of receiving pardon for my sins if I died to save this people that I wish to be the first to come forward. I am willing to strip to my shirt, bare my head, put the rope round my neck, and deliver myself into the King of England's hands." . . .
>
> Then another greatly respected and wealthy citizen, who had two beautiful daughters, stood up and said that he would go. . . . His name was Master Jean d'Aire. A third, called Master Jacques de Wissant, who owned a rich family estate, offered to accompany them. Then his brother, Master Pierre de Wissant, and a fifth and a sixth, said they would go, too.
>
> These six burghers stripped to their shirts and breeches there and then in the market-place, placed halters round their necks as had been stipulated and took the keys in their hands, each holding a bunch of them.[10]

On November 20, 1884, Rodin wrote to Omar Dewavrin, the mayor of Calais: "I just made a sketch in clay and had it cast [fig. 59]. In that way, you will be able to make a better judgment. . . . The idea seems to me completely original, from the point of view of architecture and sculpture. Nevertheless, it is the subject itself that is important and that imposes a heroic conception. The general effect of six figures sacrificing themselves is expressive and moving [expressing] patriotism, abnegation, and virtue. . . . Rarely have I succeeded in doing a sketch with so much élan and sobriety. Eustache de St. Pierre, alone, through his dignified movement, motivates and leads his relatives and friends, arm slightly raised."[11]

Two months later, on January 24, 1885, a contract between the City of Calais and Rodin was signed in which the sculptor agreed to "execute and carry through to completion . . . the idea for which he has already submitted with the model sent to the town hall of Calais." It specified that Rodin was to produce a plaster model "one-third the final size of the monument, thoroughly worked out, finished, and completed, needing only to be enlarged and perfected" and obliged the sculptor to "incorporate in the final group any changes an examination of said model by the Committee would suggest." It was further stipulated that "after executing the plaster model, M. Rodin will follow the reproduction of his work at the founder's and will give toward this operation all the artist's care and help necessary in a similar situation until it is completely finished."[12]

But as was to occur so frequently in Rodin's career, his model provoked criticism. A note signed "a passerby," published on 2 August 1885 in the newspaper *Le Patriote*, concluded that "instead of assuming the pyramid shape generally used for this type of monument, the group forms a cube, the effect of which is most graceless." On 19 August Rodin responded that "you must agree with me in thinking that our sculpture must be treated in the national taste, that of the sublime Gothic epoch," which is characterized by "pure, powerful, and naive genius. It is for that reason, sir, that I have chosen to express my sculpture in the language of Froissart's time," further explaining, "It is for that reason I reject the pyramid, which belongs to our conventional art and which immobilizes."[13]

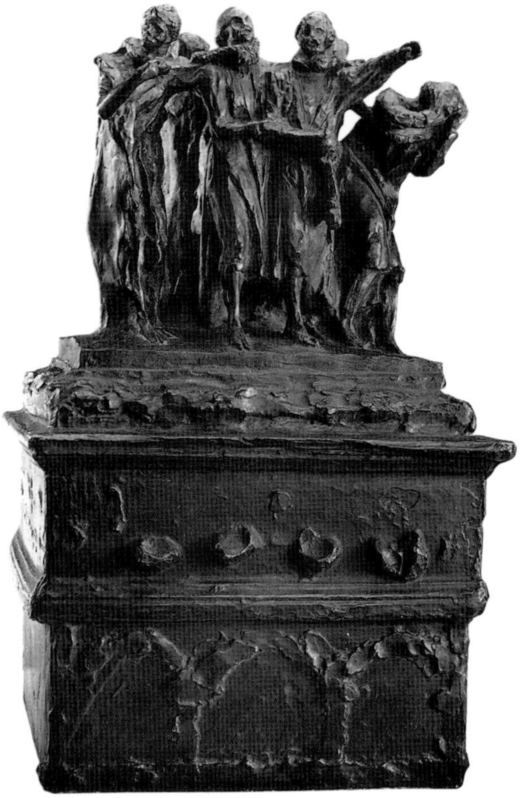

59
First Maquette for "The Burghers of Calais," 1884
Posthumous cast, 2/12
59.4 × 33 × 28.6
1974.97 (cat. 8)

Some, however, like the American sculptor Truman H. Bartlett, responded with empathic enthusiasm to Rodin's composition. In his ten-part article on the sculptor, Bartlett described the *Burghers* as "a sacrificial procession of corporeal apparitions. . . . Each figure, according to its temperament, expresses a different emotion. One goes in humble submission, another in repressing rage, while St. Pierre, the most heroic of all, grasps with trembling desperation the ribbon upon which are strung the keys of Calais' gates, raises his head in contemptuous defiance, and stretches up like a proud saint, fit to face all the conquerors. None of these statues is godlike, but they are intensely, and almost brutally human. Great, all the same, because they are men of their day, of today, and will be forever. Nor do they seem to feel for themselves as individuals, they go as a self-sacrificing answer against human cruelty, crying out like giants."[14]

As the project matured, Rodin wrote in December 1893 to Dewavrin about a revised plan to eliminate the traditional pedestal, which the Calais committee did not accept: "I had thought that, placed very low, the group would become more intimate and would allow the public to enter into the drama of misery and of sacrifice."[15] As he later explained to the writer Paul Gsell, he had wished "to have my statues placed one behind the other . . . on the very paving of the square . . . like a living rosary of suffering and sacrifice. . . . My figures would so have appeared to walk from the municipal hall to the camp of Edward III. The people of Calais of today, who would have been almost elbow to elbow with them, would have felt the tradition of solidarity that ties them to these heroes. . . . But my proposal was rejected, and a graceless, unnecessary pedestal was forced on me. They were mistaken, I am sure."[16]

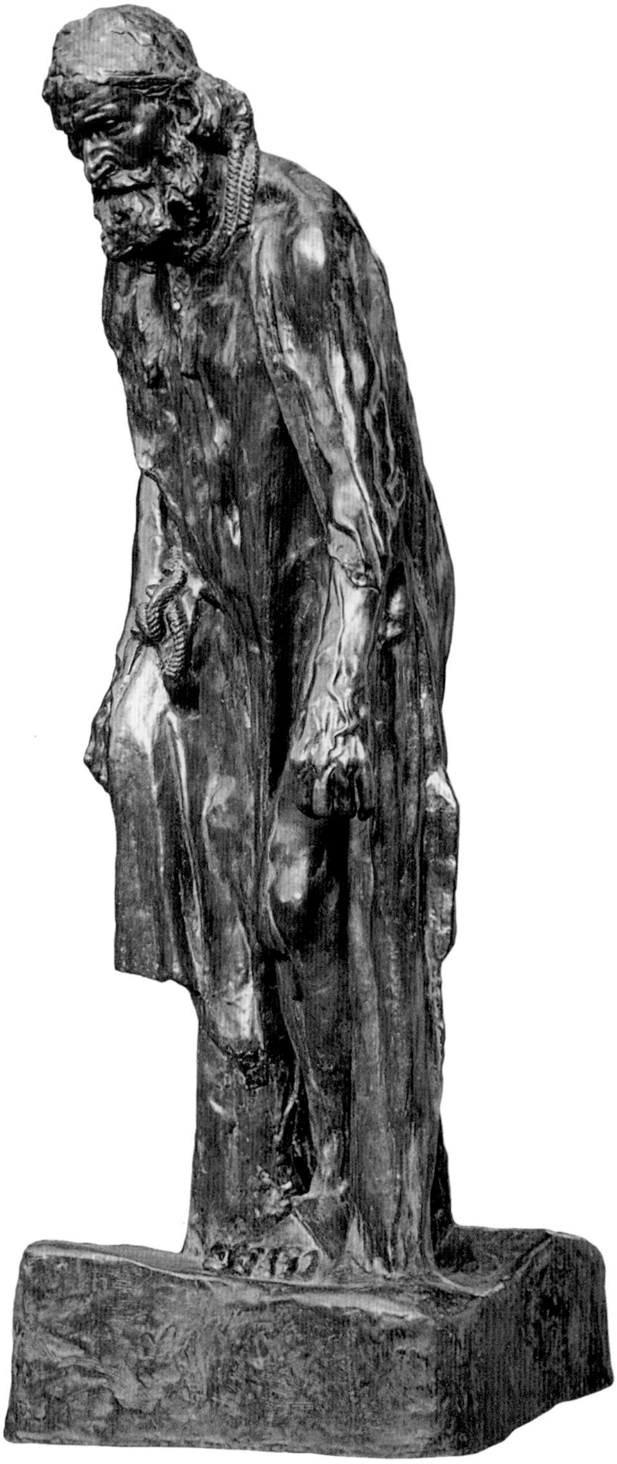

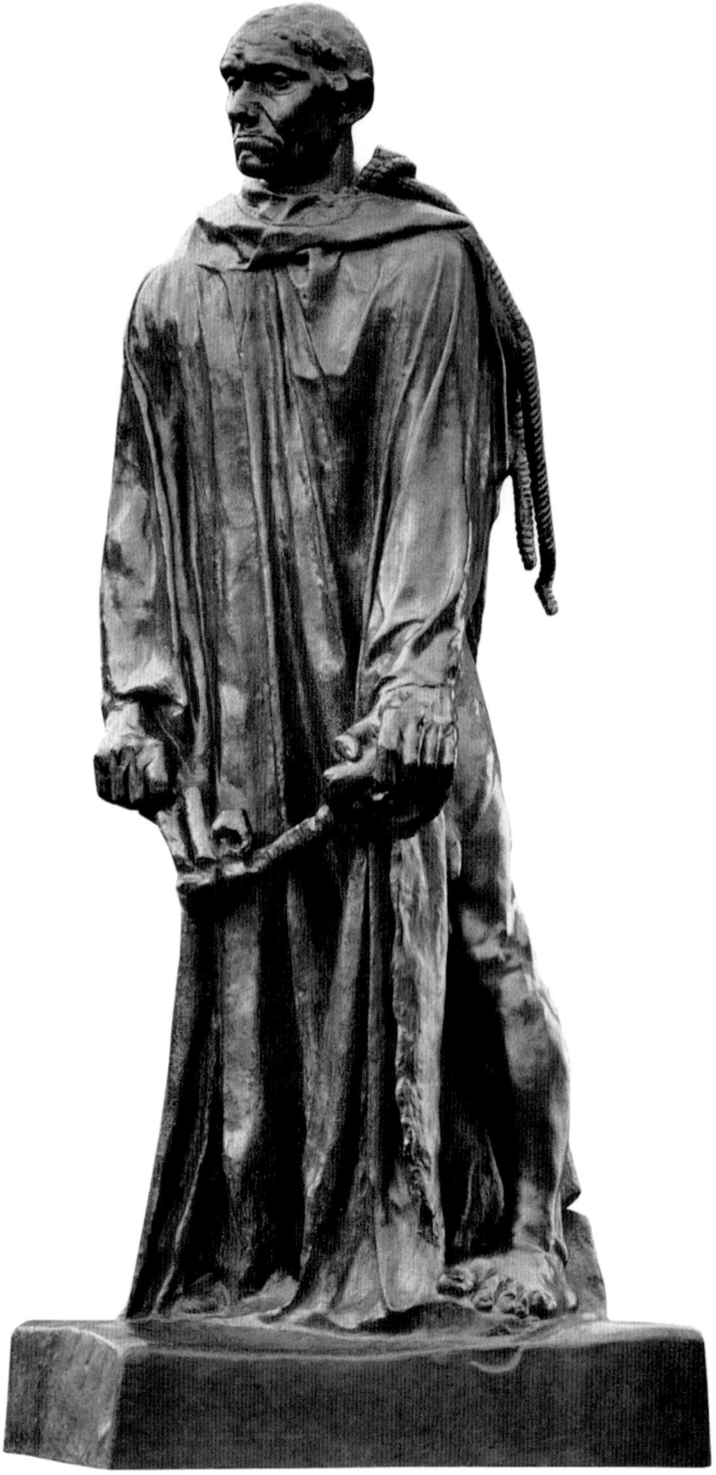

60

[ABOVE LEFT]

Eustache de Saint-Pierre, Final Version, 1885–86

Cast 1981, 2/12

220.2 × 77.7 × 124.3

1992.145 (cat. 13)

61

[ABOVE RIGHT]

Jean d'Aire, Final Version, 1886

Cast 1982, 1/4

218.4 × 86.3 × 88.9

1992.164 (cat. 19)

62

[OPPOSITE LEFT]

Andrieu d'Andres, Final Version, c. 1886–87

Cast 1981, 2/12

200.7 × 83.8 × 129.5

1992.162 (cat. 23)

63

[OPPOSITE RIGHT]

Jacques de Wissant, Final Version, c. 1886–88

Cast 1987, 2/4

210.8 × 118.1 × 68.6

1992.185 (cat. 25)

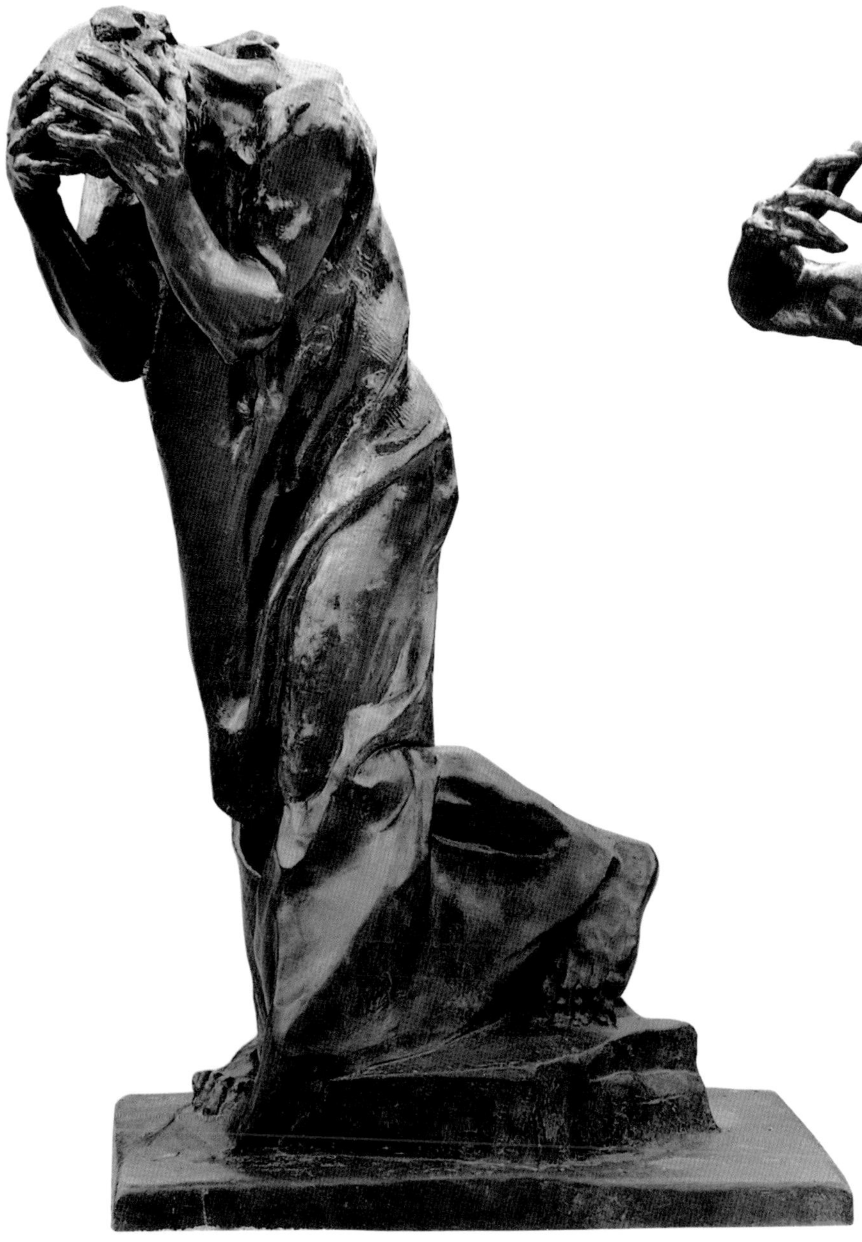
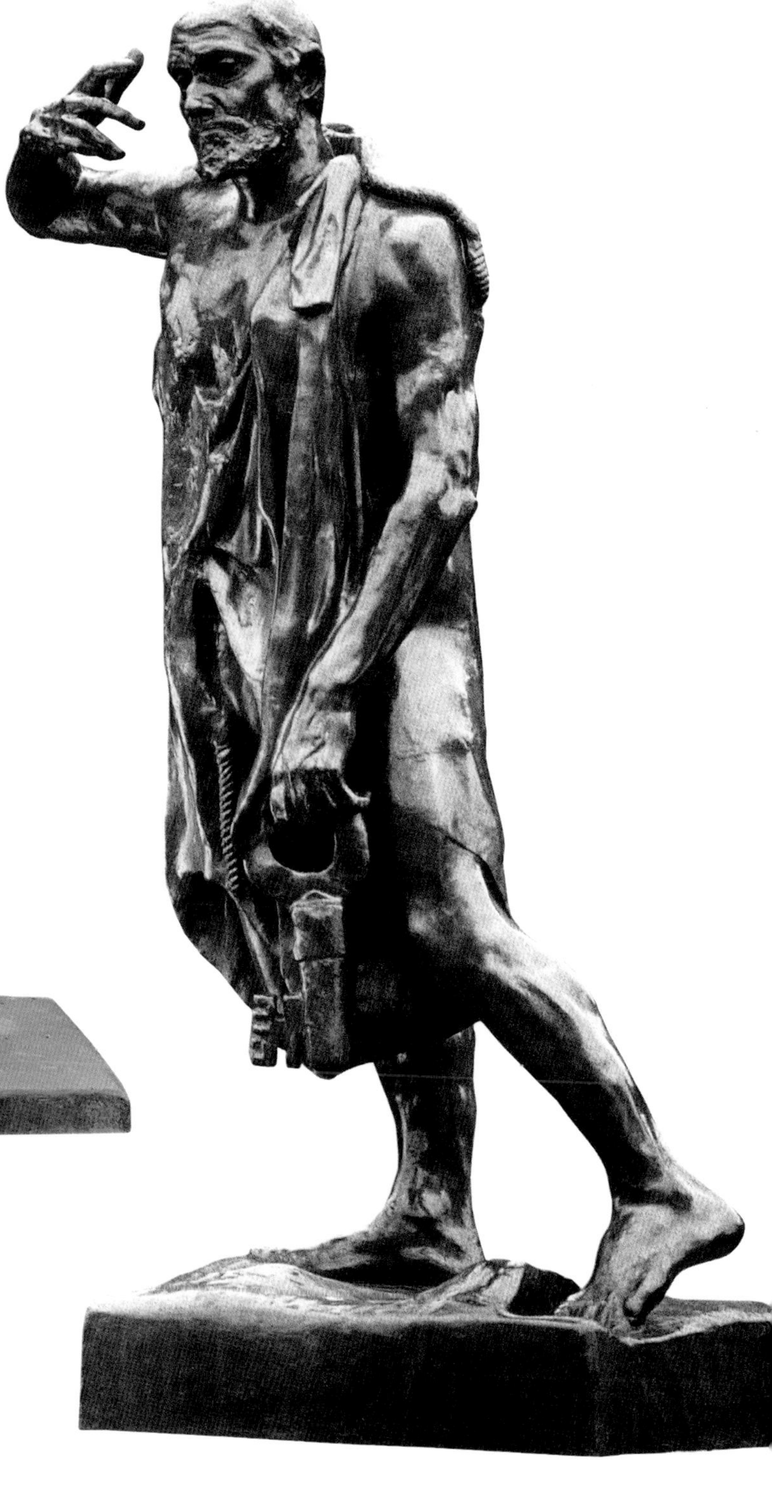

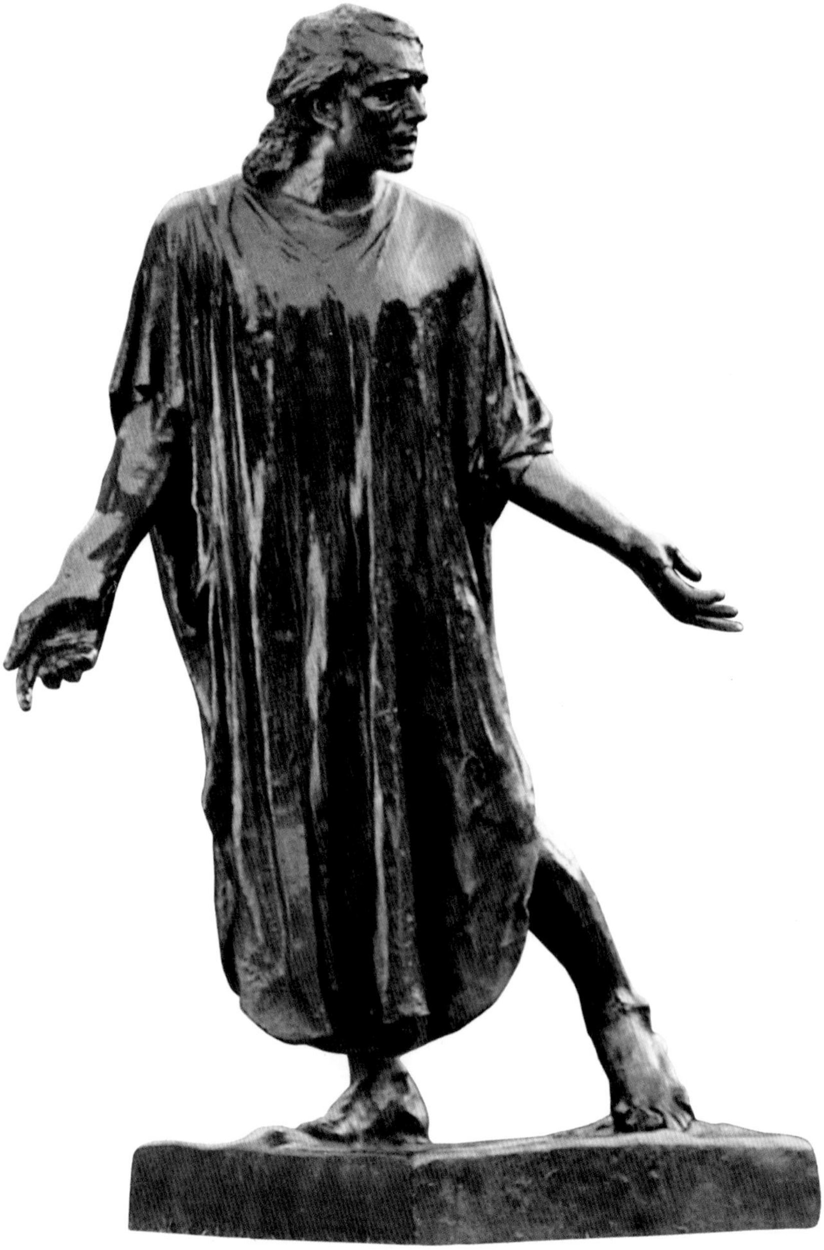

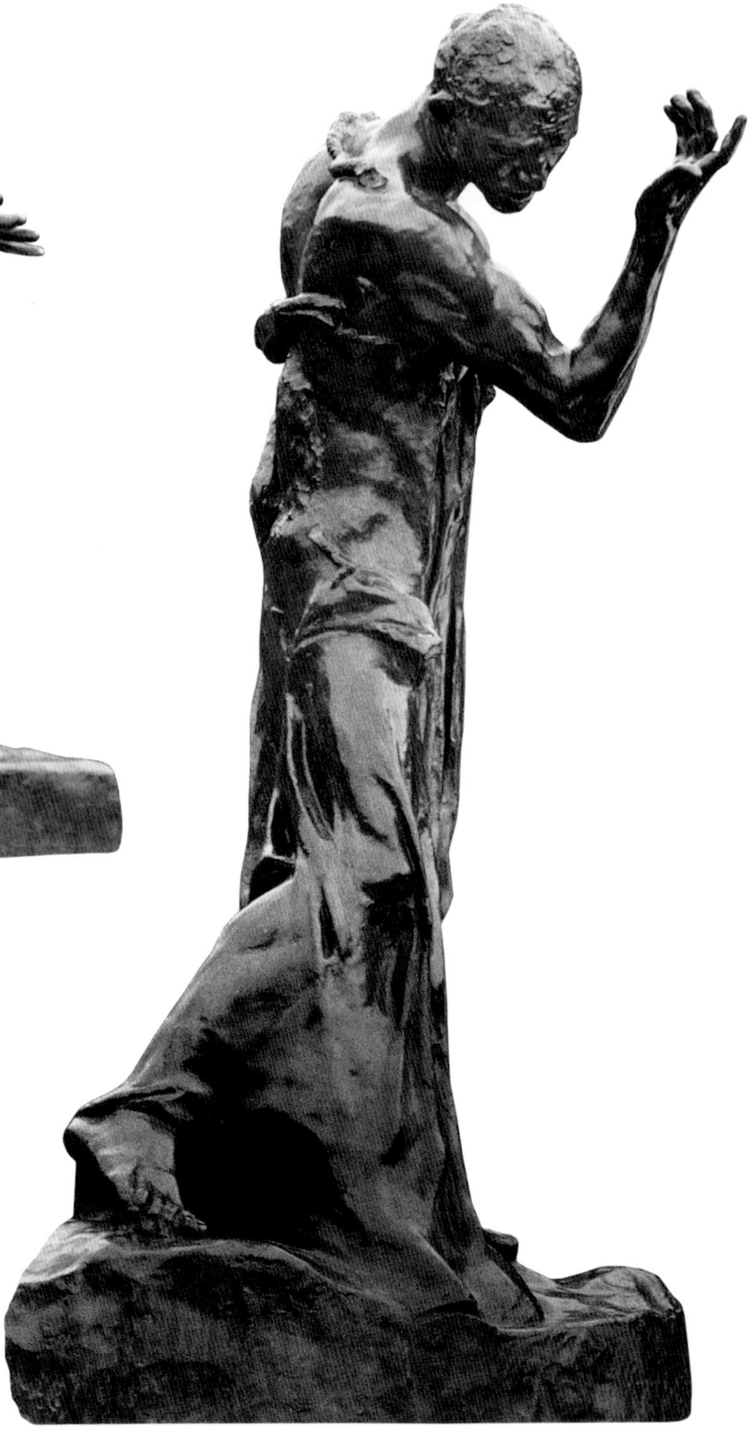

As late as 1914, Rodin was still compelled to explain the figures, which had been modeled a quarter century earlier.

> I did not hesitate to make them as thin and weak as possible. If, in order to respect some academic convention or other, I had tried to show bodies that were still agreeable to look at I would have betrayed my subject. These people, having passed through the privations of a long siege, no longer have anything but skin on their bones. The more frightful my representation of them, the more people should praise me for knowing how to show the truth of history. I have not shown them grouped in a triumphant apotheosis; such a glorification of their heroism would not have corresponded to anything real. On the contrary, I have, as it were, threaded them one behind the other, because in the indecision of the last inner combat which ensues, between their devotion to their cause and their fear of dying, each of them is isolated in front of his conscience. They are still questioning themselves to know if they have the strength to accomplish the supreme sacrifice—their soul pushes them onward, but their feet refuse to walk. They drag themselves along painfully, as much because of the feebleness to which famine has reduced them as because of the terrifying nature of the sacrifice. And certainly, if I have succeeded in showing how much the body, weakened by the most cruel sufferings, still holds on to life, how much power it still has over the spirit that is consumed with bravery, I can congratulate myself on not having remained beneath the noble theme I dealt with. I did not want a pedestal for these figures. I wanted them to be placed on, even affixed to, the paving stones of the square in front of the Hôtel de Ville in Calais so that it looked as if they were leaving in order to go to the enemy camp. In this way they would have been, as it were, mixed with the daily life of the town: passersby would have elbowed them, and they would have felt through this contact the emotion of the living past in their midst; they would have said to themselves: "Our ancestors are our neighbors and our models, and the day when it will be granted to us to imitate their example, we would show that we have not degenerated from it." . . . But the commissioning body understood nothing of the desires I expressed. They thought I was mad . . . Statues without a pedestal! Where had that ever been seen before? There must be a pedestal; there was no way of getting around it.[17]

Five years after receiving the contract from Calais, Rodin completed the full-scale monument in plaster, which was displayed in his 1889 exhibition shared with the Impressionist painter Claude Monet. In this configuration the six gaunt figures occupy a single low plinth. Shrewdly recognizing that individual figures would have greater market potential than the large multi-figure composition, Rodin reworked bases and sometimes sent solitary

64
[OPPOSITE LEFT]
Jean de Fiennes, Final Version, 1885–86
Cast 1981, 1/12
212.4 × 124.3 × 98.4
1992.147 (cat. 28)

65
[OPPOSITE RIGHT]
Pierre de Wissant, Final Version, c. 1886–87
Cast 1981, 6/12
209.8 × 103.6 × 124.3
1992.148 (cat. 30)

Burghers to international exhibitions, making casts available to collectors and museums. Stanford's *Burghers of Calais* is made up of the six individual figures (figs. 60–65). Appropriately on display in Memorial Court, which is dedicated to students who fell in World War I, they are configured as an expanded version of the single-base composition. Occupying the same relative positions, these exemplars of civic virtue are set among cobblestones and low to the ground to approximate the sculptor's often-expressed intentions for their display.

The Monument to Honoré de Balzac

FROM PORTRAIT TO SYMBOL

On 14 August 1891 the author Emile Zola wrote to Rodin informing him that following the death of Henri Chapu, to whom the commission had originally been given, "the Committee of the Société des Gens de Lettres ... selected you by twelve votes against eight to execute the statue of Balzac, which is to be erected on the Square of the Palais Royal."[18] This initiated a seven-year creative struggle that involved archival research and dozens of experimental figures and portraits. When Rodin finally displayed the results of his efforts in 1889, the Société, which had anticipated "a superb statue" representing the author of *The Human Comedy* (*La Comédie humaine*), was disappointed and rejected Rodin's startling and novel representation of the great novelist (fig. 66). The city government even withdrew its offer of a public site, but this decision was reversed in 1939, when a bronze cast was installed in Paris.

Creating a monument to Balzac (1799–1850) challenged Rodin in a variety of ways. First, the sculptor habitually worked from live subjects, but the writer had died forty-one years prior to the commission. To compensate for this problem, Rodin read literary descriptions of the author and gathered an extensive archive of visual data, including paintings, drawings, and caricatures (fig. 67), as well as a copy of the only known photographic portrait of Balzac (fig. 68). Rodin also visited the author's native Touraine in search of people who recalled or resembled the great novelist, and he located the author's tailor, who made a new suit to Balzac's measurements. In addition, Rodin read the *Comedy* itself in an effort to understand the writer's spirit and accomplishment. What his studies in part revealed was that physically this man—whose main activities were writing, talking, eating, and lovemaking—was an unpromising subject for a monumental sculpture and that Balzac's

66
[OPPOSITE]
Final Study for the "Monument to Honoré de Balzac," c. 1897
Cast 1976, 12/12
110.5 × 43.2 × 38.1
1992.168 (cat. 112)

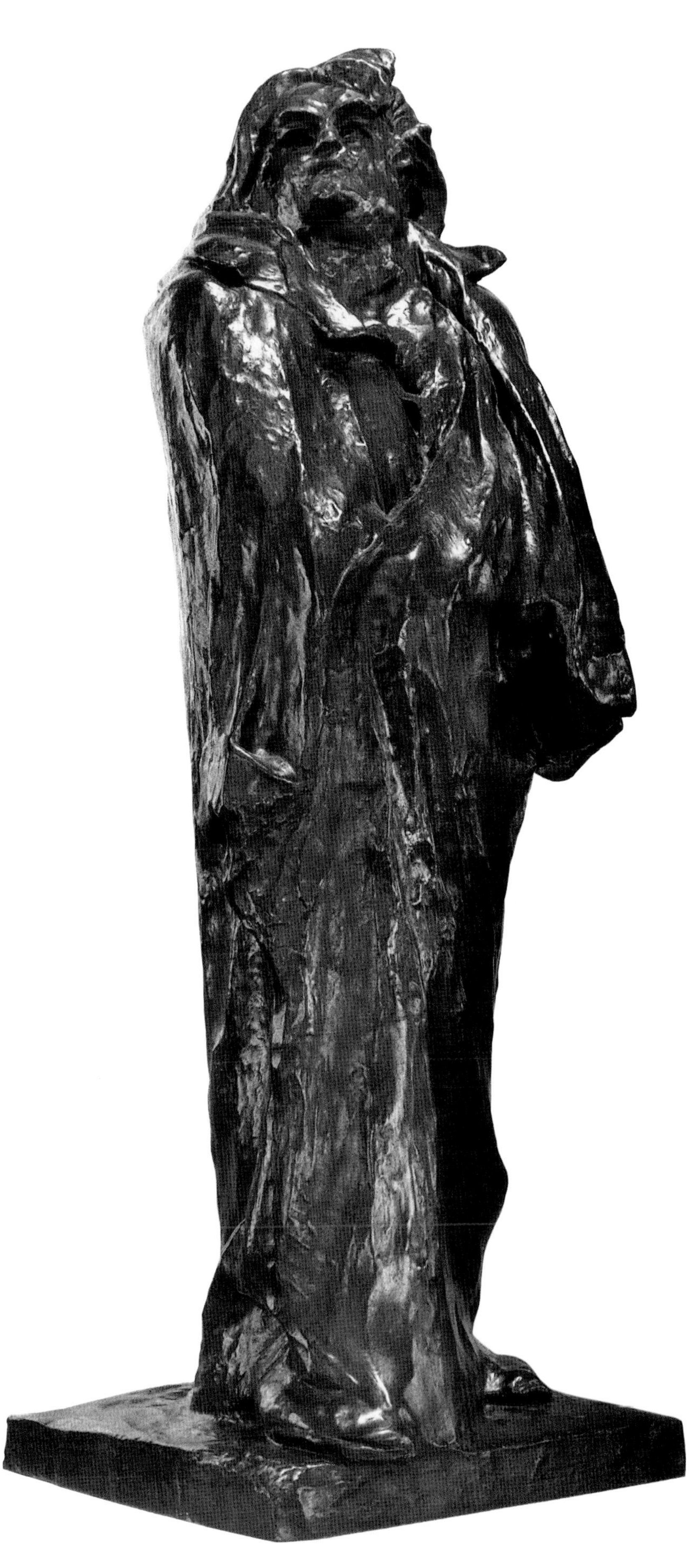

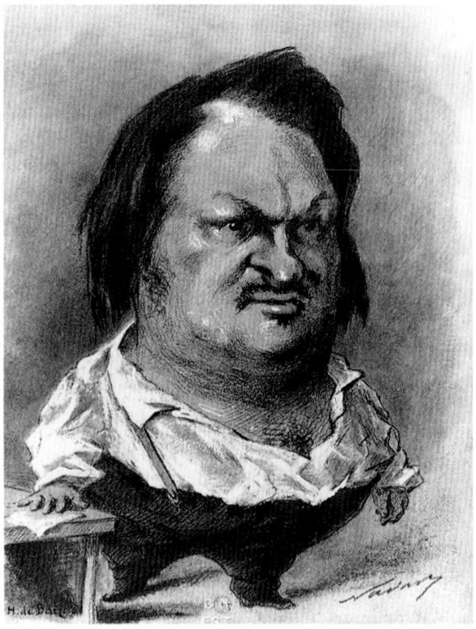

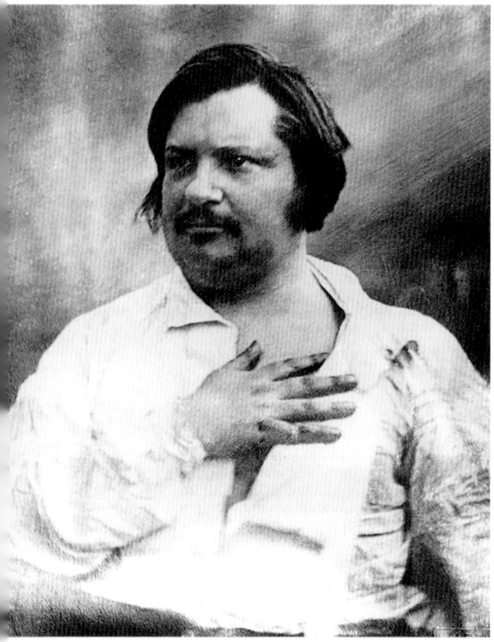

67
[TOP]
Nadar (Félix Tournachon) (1820–1910)
Caricature of Honoré de Balzac, c. 1856
Charcoal with gouache
Collection Bibliothèque Nationale, Paris

68
[BOTTOM]
Louis-Auguste Bisson (1826–1900)
Honoré de Balzac, 1842
Daguerreotype
6.7 × 8.2
Collection Maison de Balzac, Paris

physique and physiognomy were too well known to be altogether ignored. That people knew Balzac had been a short, corpulent man with unruly hair, fat hands, brilliant eyes, an animated manner of speaking, and an intelligent and highly expressive face was necessarily daunting for a sculptor who preferred to work from nature and on principle rejected allegory as an alternative to portraiture.

The eleven Balzac casts in the Stanford collection suggest the dozens of experiments in body type, pose, and expression that Rodin undertook (figs. 69, 70).[19] Although the committee, as well as many reviewers, condemned his solution to the problem, artists as different as Claude Monet and Paul Cézanne praised the statue, which was a revelation to many. For example, the young Edward Steichen was inspired to travel to France after seeing a photograph of the rejected statue in a Milwaukee newspaper. Except for the thick neck, Rodin too was essentially satisfied, as he explained in an article that appeared in *Le Journal* on 12 May 1898, the day following the committee's rejection of the statue at the Salon:

> I sought in Balzac . . . to render in sculpture what was not photographic. One can find errors in my Balzac: the artist does not always realize his dream: but I believe in the truth of my principle: and Balzac, rejected or not, is none the less in the line of demarcation between commercial sculpture and the art of sculpture. . . . My principle is to imitate not only form but also life. I search in nature for this life and amplify it by exaggerating the holes and lumps, to gain thereby more light, after which I search for a synthesis of the whole. . . . I am now too old to defend my art, which has sincerity as its defense.[20]

Still assessing the significance of *Balzac* nine years later, Rodin was able to explain in greater detail what he had intended to express:

> I had to show a Balzac in his study, breathless, hair in disorder, eyes lost in a dream, a genius who in his little room reconstructs piece by piece all of society in order to bring it into tumultuous life before his contemporaries and generations to come; Balzac truly heroic who does not stop to rest for a moment, who makes night into day, who drives himself in vain to fill the gaps made by his debts, who above all dedicates himself to building an immortal monument, who is transported by passion, whose body is made frenetic and violent and who does not heed the warnings of his diseased heart from which he will soon die. It seems to me that such a Balzac, even, seen in a public place would be greater and more worthy of admiration than just any writer who sits in a chair or who proudly poses for the enthusiastic crowd. In sum, there is nothing more beautiful than the absolute truth or real existence.[21]

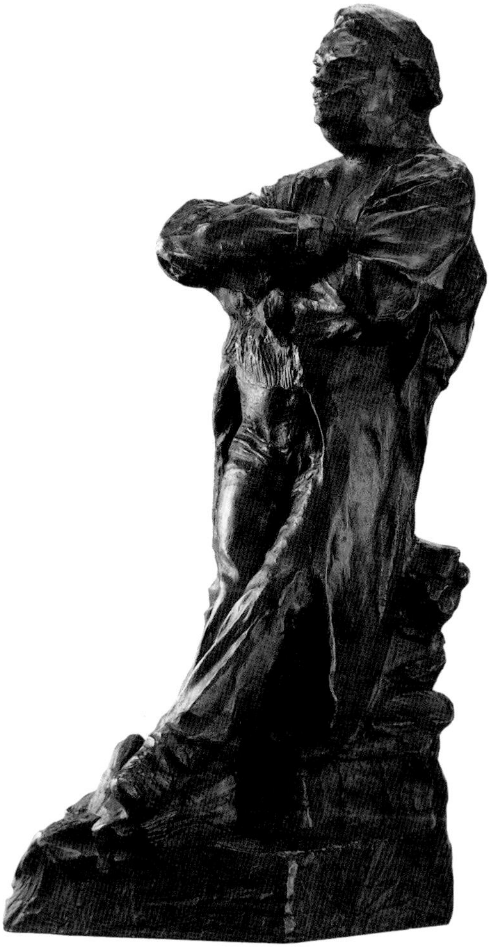

69

[ABOVE]

Honoré de Balzac in a Frock Coat, c. 1891–92
Cast 1976, 7/12
59.7 × 24.1 × 29.8
1974.91 (cat. 102)

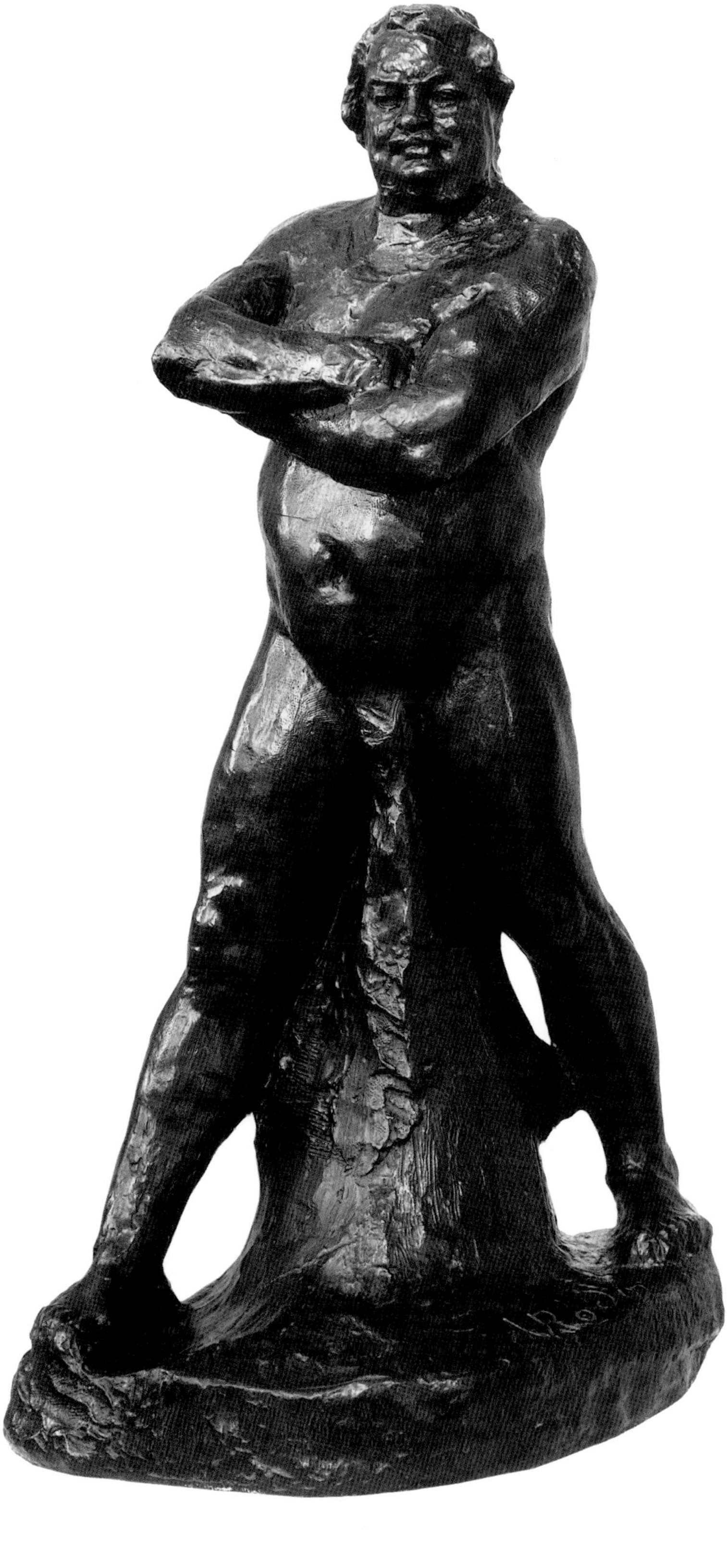

70

[RIGHT]

Nude Honoré de Balzac with Folded Arms, 1892–93
Cast 1968, 1/12
127.6 × 52.1 × 82.9
1974.89 (cat. 109)

Of course, had he seen the statue, Balzac, with his exceptional capacity for description, would have been able to find words to characterize the intellectual drama of this unparalleled work. He would have been able to convey a sense of the vitality that is barely contained within the robe habitually worn by the author and the imaginative prowess that seems almost to burst from the powerful head, with its penetrating gaze. But for others the impact of the figure may be most effectively expressed in yet other images, such as the interpretive photographs Steichen took with the encouragement of the sculptor (see fig. 23).

Notes

1. The collection also includes a bronze of the "large" (H: 39 in.) reduction and a plaster of the "small" (H: 26 in.) reduction, both dating from 1903–4 (Albert E. Elsen with Rosalyn Frankel Jamison, *Rodin's Art: The Rodin Collection of the Iris and Gerald Cantor Center for Visual Arts at Stanford University*, ed. Bernard Barryte [New York: Oxford University Press, 2003], cat. 1–3).

2. The first phrase comes from Charles Timbal's review of the 1877 Paris Salon (*Gazette des beaux-arts*, July 1877), the second from Charles Frémine's review of the 1883 Exposition des arts libéraux (*Le Rappel*, 28 November 1883), where *The Age of Bronze* was again exhibited; both are reprinted in Ruth Butler, ed., *Rodin in Perspective* (Englewood Cliffs, N.J.: Prentice-Hall, 1980), 35, 42.

3. For an introduction to these drawings, see Claudie Judrin, *Rodin: Hell and Paradise: Sculptor's Drawings* (Paris: Musée Rodin, 2002), 16–22.

4. Truman H. Bartlett, "Auguste Rodin, Sculptor," *American Architect and Building News* 25, no. 689 (1889), reprinted in *Auguste Rodin: Readings on His Life and Art*, ed. Albert Elsen (Englewood Cliffs, N.J.: Prentice-Hall, 1965), 69, 73.

5. Rodin's plaster versions of the *Gates* are on view at the Musée Rodin and the Musée d'Orsay in Paris. In addition to the example at Stanford, bronze casts are located at the Musée Rodin, Paris; Rodin Museum, Philadelphia; Kunsthaus, Zurich; Rodin Gallery, Seoul; Prefectural Museum of Art, Shizuoka, Japan; and National Museum of Western Art, Tokyo.

6. Rainer Maria Rilke, *Rodin*, trans. Jesse Lemont and Hans Trausil (New York: Fine Editions Press, 1945), reprinted in *Auguste Rodin: Readings on His Life and Art*, ed. Albert Elsen (Englewood Cliffs, N.J.: Prentice-Hall, 1965), 113.

7. Henri-Charles-Etienne Dujardin-Beaumetz, "Rodin's Reflections on Art," in Elsen, ed., *Auguste Rodin*, 171.

8. With changes to its arms, the figure also became part of the marble couple *Orpheus and Eurydice* (New York, Metropolitan Museum of Art).

9. Auguste Rodin, *Art: Conversations with Paul Gsell* (1911), trans. Jacques de Caso and Patricia B. Sanders (Berkeley: University of California Press, 1984), 68.

10. Jean Froissart, *Chronicles*, ed. and trans. Geoffrey Brereton (Harmondsworth, England: Penguin Books, 1968), 106–8.

11. Claudie Judrin et al., *Auguste Rodin: "Le Monument des bourgeois de Calais" (1884–95)*, exh. cat. (Calais: Musée des Beaux-Arts, 1977), 41–42; translated in Elsen, *Rodin's Art*, 69.

12. The contract is translated in Mary Jo McNamara and Albert Elsen, *Rodin's "Burghers of Calais,"* exh. cat., Stanford Art Gallery (New York: Cantor, Fitzgerald Group, 1977), 68.

13. Cited in Elsen, *Rodin's Art*, 77–79.

14. Bartlett, "Auguste Rodin, Sculptor," 82.

15. Rodin to Dewavrin, 8 December 1893, cited in Elsen, *Rodin's Art*, 85.

16. Rodin, *Art: Conversations with Paul Gsell*, 38–39.

17. Paul Gsell, "Chez Rodin," *L'Art et les artistes*, no. 106 (April 1914): 66–67, trans. in John L. Tancock, *The Sculpture of Auguste Rodin* (Philadelphia: Philadelphia Museum of Art, 1976), 388, 390.

18. Cited in Frederick Lawton, *The Life and Work of Auguste Rodin* (New York: Charles Scribner's Sons, 1907), 176.

19. See Elsen, *Rodin's Art*, 353–412, and especially Antoinette Le Normand-Romain, ed., *1898: Le "Balzac" de Rodin*, exh. cat. Musée Rodin (Paris, 1998).

20. Translated in Elsen, *Rodin's Art*, 382.

21. Paul Gsell, "Chez Rodin," *L'Art et les artistes*, no. 23 (4 February 1907), 410–11, translated in Elsen, *Rodin's Art*, 384.

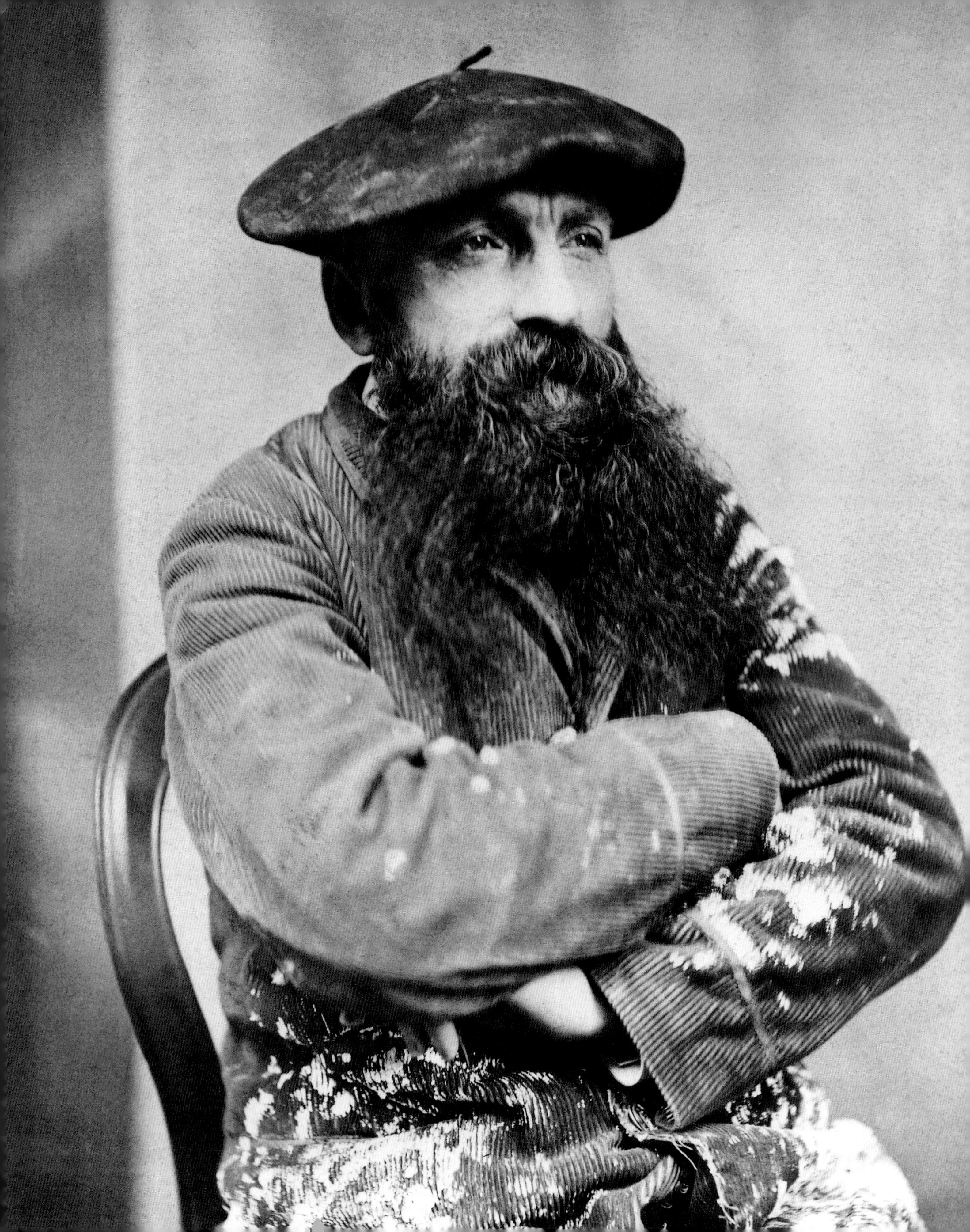

Rodin on Art

On Portraiture

If the artist only reproduces the superficial features like a photographer, if he exactly records the diverse features of a physiognomy, but without relating these to character, he does not deserve our admiration. The resemblance he should achieve is that of the soul. Only this matters. This is what the sculptor or the painter must seek behind the mask. In a word, every feature must be *expressive*; it must help reveal the psyche. . . . To tell the truth, there is no artistic work that requires as much penetrating insight as the bust and the portrait. People sometimes believe that the profession of the artist demands more manual skill than intelligence. It suffices to look at a good bust to redress this error. Such a work is the equivalent of a biography. Houdon's busts, for instance, are written like chapters of memoirs. Period, ancestry, profession, personal character—everything is indicated. [Rodin, *Art: Conversations with Paul Gsell*, 54–55]

On Expression

And even in those of my works in which action is less stressed, I have always sought to include some indication of gesture; it is very rare that I have represented complete repose. I have always tried to express the interior

71
[OPPOSITE]
Photographer unknown
Rodin with Arms Crossed, 1880
Albumen print
21.8 × 16.8
Collection Musée Rodin, Paris

feelings through the mobility of the muscles. Even in my busts I have often given some inclination, some deviation, some expressive direction in order to enhance the meaning of the physiognomy. . . . First, note that *movement is the transition from one attitude to another*. This simple statement, which sounds like a truism, is indeed the key to the mystery. You have certainly read in Ovid how Daphne was transformed into a laurel. . . . The charming writer shows the body . . . being covered with bark . . . so that . . . one still sees the woman that will soon cease to be and the sapling . . . she will become. . . . It is basically a metamorphosis of this kind that the painter or sculptor executes in making his personages move. He makes visible the passage of one pose into the other; he indicates how imperceptibly the first glides into the second. In his work, one still detects a part of what was while one discovers in part what will be. [Rodin, *Art: Conversations with Paul Gsell*, 27–29]

On Movement in Art and Photography

Now take my *Saint John* [*the Baptist Preaching*] (see fig. 15). He is represented with two feet on the ground, but a high-speed photograph of a model moving in the same way would probably show the back foot already raised and moving forward. Or, on the other hand, the forward foot would not yet be on the ground if the back leg in the photograph occupied the same position as in my statue. For just this reason this photographed model would present the bizarre appearance of a man suddenly struck with paralysis and petrified in his pose. . . . In high-speed photographs, although figures are caught in full action, they seem suddenly frozen in mid-air. This is because every part of their body is reproduced exactly at the same twentieth or fortieth of a second, and there is not, as in art, the gradual unfolding of a movement. . . . It is the artist who tells the truth and photography that lies. For in reality, time does not stand still. And if the artist succeeds in producing the impression of a gesture that is executed in several instants, his work is certainly much less conventional than the scientific image where time is abruptly suspended. [Rodin, *Art: Conversations with Paul Gsell*, 31–32]

On Light

The statue is transformed under the light, like everything that has volume: the atmosphere imposes successive transformations upon it. Thus it is important that the work approach closely to reality, and then the colorations arrange and distribute themselves, play upon true forms, consequently upon exact contours. Light separates, disjoins, decomposes, destroys false forms, be they rounded or thin; but when it shines on exact modeling, it gives the work the aspect and character of life. We never see anything in isolation; an object is always in rapport with what is in front, beside, behind, above, below. The relations are important. A beautiful work takes on all its strength when, in gardens or public squares, free to all the caprices of light, it affirms itself; the unity of color is added to the unity of form; all abides, all is linked together. It dominates and imposes itself, resplendent with that incomparable brilliance of the nude figure in the open air. [Dujardin-Beaumetz, *Rodin's Reflections on Art*, 170–71]

On Craft

There is no such thing as a badly executed masterpiece. A beautiful execution is the faithful copy of nature. Without her, no truth, no simplicity, no style, no unity. Without [skilled] execution, the work remains a dream, an intention, an aspiration, without affirmation or will, without real translation: whatever the subject treated may be, however common, the execution gives it life; it is only the execution which allows the artist to render the truth in its proper character. Without workmanship the work of art cannot endure, it passes with the fashions of thinking and feeling peculiar to its time. It is the perfection of craft which, giving to the thought and vision of the artist all the fullness of his expression, makes the masterpiece a constant vision of beauty. It is the expression of nature, rendered by the genius of the artist, which gives to his works that calm serenity—powerful, victorious—and creates around it that atmosphere of peace which emanates from the beautiful. . . . It is important that the artist be really master of his métier, that he consecrate all his resources to giving it its total expression; in a word, that he give back to the material he uses all of which it is susceptible. [Dujardin-Beaumetz, *Rodin's Reflections on Art*, 174]

On the Limits of Reason

To judge a work of art with the logical precision of a philosophical premise or the analyses of experimental science is a fundamental error. It is even difficult to talk about it. When music is talked of, one is always tempted to interrupt the conversation and say, "Let's go listen to it," or of sculpture or painting, "Let's look." Art contains some expressions which could not be exactly demonstrated by reason. The artist's sensibility shows him beauties in nature which go beyond what his intelligence alone could have conceived. The artist makes tangible that which was invisible. [Dujardin-Beaumetz, *Rodin's Reflections on Art*, 177]

On Drawing

The greatest difficulty that one encounters in art, that which must be surmounted before everything else and which dominates all others, comes from the necessity of drawing well; only the knowledge of drawing permits one to compare, judge, express simplicity in fixing the essential. By means of drawing, the work takes on the power of natural things; without drawing, no truth. Thus it is important to exert the mind and eye constantly to see, to understand in order to render well. Study by contours is a magnificent tool; but it demands great mental tension to render in all their character and truth the multiple forms which it shows successively. In order to render the contours, one must follow nature with tireless patience and determination. I may add that the will to follow nature exactly develops taste, exercises the reason, shows wisdom. It gives calm within strength, serenity within the fullness of expression of life. [Dujardin-Beaumetz, *Rodin's Reflections on Art*, 161]

On the Partial Figure

I am an inventor. . . . I deliver the results of my researches in morceaux which are the study of planes and modeling. I am reproached for not personally showing all the applications which result from them. Let those who follow me occupy themselves with this task. I must content myself with having led the intelligence of the artist of my time into the environment of Michelangelo and the Antique. . . . A well made torso contains all of life. One doesn't add anything by joining arms and legs to it. My morceaux are the examples that I propose for the study of other artists. They are not finished, one says. And the cathedrals, are they finished? [Judith Cladel, *Rodin: L'oeuvre et l'homme* (Brussels: Van Oest, 1908), 98]

On Art's Purpose

The aim of art is not to copy literally. It consists in slightly exaggerating the character of the model in order to make it salient; it consists also in re-assembling in a single expression the successive expressions given by the same model. Art is the living synthesis. [Judith Cladel, *Rodin: The Man and His Art with Leaves from His Note-Book* (New York: Century, 1918), 218]

On Beauty

Beauty is everywhere. It is not that Beauty fails to come before our eyes but that our eyes fail to perceive it. Beauty is character and expression. Now, there is nothing in nature that has more character than the human body. It evokes through its strength or its grace the most varied images. At one moment, it resembles a flower: the bending of the torso imitates the stem, while the smile of the breast, head, and gleaming hair correspond to the blooming of the corolla. At another moment, it recalls a supple liana. . . . Another time, the human body curved back is like . . . a beautiful bow from which Eros aims his invisible arrows. Yet another time it is an urn. I have often had a model sit on the floor and turn her back to me with her arms and legs drawn before her. In this position, only the silhouette of the back . . . appears, and this forms a vase with an exquisite contour: the amphora that holds the life of the future in its flanks. The human body is above all the mirror of the soul, and from this comes its greatest beauty. [Rodin, *Art: Conversations with Paul Gsell*, 51–52]

On Decorative Art

For more than a century, what is called fine art has been separated from the crafts. As if art were not a great entity! How detestable is the current expression "decorative art." All art is decorative. [Dujardin-Beaumetz, *Rodin's Reflections on Art*, 151]

On Art and Ugliness

Now for the great artist, everything in Nature has "character," for the uncompromising frankness of his observation penetrates the hidden meaning of everything. And that which is considered "ugly" in Nature often presents more "character" than what is called beautiful because in the contortion of a sickly physiognomy, in the scoring of a vicious mask, in every deformity, in every blemish the inner truth bursts forth more easily than from regular and wholesome features. And since it is solely the power of "character" that creates beauty in Art, it often happens that the one who is the most ugly in Nature is the most beautiful in Art. There is nothing "ugly" in Art except that which is without "character," that is to say, that which has neither outer nor inner truth. The ugly in Art is that which is false; that which is artificial; that which seeks to be pretty or beautiful, instead of being expressive; that which is affected and precious; that which smiles without motive; that which is pretentious without reason . . . all that is without soul and truth; all that is only a parade of beauty and grace; all that lies. When an artist, intending to embellish Nature . . . tones down the grimace of pain, the deterioration of old age, the hideousness of perversity; when he organizes Nature, softens it, disguises it, tempers it to please the ignorant public; he creates ugliness because he is afraid of the truth. For an artist worthy of the name, everything is beautiful in Nature because his eyes . . . read in Nature . . . as from an open book, every internal truth. He has only to look at a human face to decipher a soul; no feature fools him. Hypocrisy is for him as transparent as sincerity. . . . the slightest knitting of the brows, a fleeting look reveal to him the secrets of the heart. [Rodin, *Art: Conversations with Paul Gsell*, 19–20]

On Inspiration

Even in suffering, even in the death of loved ones, and even in the betrayal of a friend, the great artist—by whom I mean the poet, as well as the painter and the sculptor—finds the tragic pleasure of admiration. Sometimes his heart is tortured, but even more strongly than the suffering, he feels the bitter joy of understanding and expressing. . . . He regards his own anguish, his worst wounds with the enthusiasm of a man who divines the decrees of fate. Deceived by someone dear, he staggers from the blow. Then, steadying himself, he contemplates the perfidious one as a beautiful example of baseness. He greets ingratitude as an experience that enriches his soul . . . When he perceives people who destroy one another, youth that fades, vigor that flags, genius that burns out . . . he enjoys knowing, and, satiated with truth, he is formidably happy. [Rodin, *Art: Conversations with Paul Gsell*, 20–21]

On Distortion and Expression

If my modeling is bad . . . if I make faults in the anatomy, if I interpret movements poorly, if I ignore the science of animating marble, these critics are right a hundred times. But if my figures are correct and full of life, then what do they criticize? . . . What do they complain about if . . . I offer them ideas, and if I enrich forms capable of seducing the eye with signification? Furthermore, it is certainly wrong to imagine that true artists can be content with being skillful workers and do not need intelligence. On the contrary, it is indispensable to them even in painting or in carving the images that seem the most devoid of spiritual ambitions and that are only destined to charm the eye. When a good sculptor models a statue, whatever it represents, he must first conceive the general movement forcefully. Then . . . he must keep his idea for the entire composition strongly and clearly in mind. In this way, he can always compare and closely relate the smallest details of his work to it. And this is not done without an enormous amount of thinking. [Rodin, *Art: Conversations with Paul Gsell*, 69–70]

On Literary Themes

When a literary subject is so well known, the artist can treat it without fear of not being understood. Still it is better, in my opinion, for the works of painters and sculptors to contain their entire interest in themselves. Art, indeed, can provide thinking and dreaming without having any recourse to literature. Instead of illustrating scenes from poems, art should only use very clear symbols that do not rely on any written text. This has generally been my method. [Rodin, *Art: Conversations with Paul Gsell*, 73]

On Form and Expression

The form created should only provide a pretext for the emotion to expand indefinitely. . . . But to tell the truth, everything is idea, everything is symbol. So the form and poses of a human being necessarily reveal the feelings of his soul. The body always expresses the spirit for which it is the shell. And for him who has eyes to see, nudity offers the richest meaning. . . . A simple torso—calm, well-balanced, radiant with strength and grace—can make him think of the all-powerful reason that governs the world. [Rodin, *Art: Conversations with Paul Gsell*, 74–76]

RECOMMENDED READING

The following selection offers an introduction to the vast literature on Rodin. This includes reminiscences and criticism by his contemporaries, biographies, monographs, articles, and exhibition and collection catalogues. Foremost among these materials are the numerous publications of the Musée Rodin, Paris. These include comprehensive studies of individual works and of Rodin's relationships with contemporary artists, writers, and photographers; investigations of facets of the sculptor's career; an edition of his correspondence; and catalogues of the Musée's holdings, which include Rodin's drawings, his own sculpture, and his collections of ancient, Asian, and European art.

Butler, Ruth. *Rodin in Perspective*. Englewood Cliffs, N.J.: Prentice-Hall, 1980.

———. *Rodin: The Shape of Genius*. New Haven: Yale University Press, 1993.

De Caso, Jacques, and Patricia B. Sanders. *Rodin's Sculpture: A Critical Study of the Spreckels Collection*. San Francisco: Fine Arts Museums, 1977.

Descharnes, Robert, and J. E. Chabrun. *Auguste Rodin*. New York: Viking, 1967.

Dujardin-Beaumetz, Henri-Charles-Etienne. "Rodin's Reflections on Art." Translated by Ann McGarell. In *Readings on Rodin: His Life and Work*, edited by Albert Elsen, 145–85. Englewood Cliffs, N.J.: Prentice-Hall, 1965. Originally published as *Entretiens avec Rodin* (Paris: Paul Dupont, 1913).

Elsen, Albert. *Rodin*. Exhibition catalogue. New York: Museum of Modern Art, 1963.

———. *In Rodin's Studio*. Ithaca, N.Y.: Cornell University Press, 1980.

———. *"The Gates of Hell" by Auguste Rodin*. Stanford, Calif.: Stanford University Press, 1985.

———, ed. *Readings on Rodin: His Life and Work*. Englewood Cliffs, N.J.: Prentice-Hall, 1965.

———, ed. *Rodin Rediscovered*. Exhibition catalogue. Washington, D.C.: National Gallery of Art, 1981.

Elsen, Albert, with Rosalyn Frankel Jamison. *Rodin's Art: The Rodin Collection of the Iris and B. Gerald Cantor Center for Visual Arts, Stanford University*. New York: Oxford University Press, 2003.

Le Normand-Romain, Antoinette. *The Gates of Hell*. Translated by Allan Howard. Paris: Musée Rodin, 1999.

Rodin, Auguste. *Art: Conversations with Paul Gsell*. Translated by Jacques de Caso and Patricia B. Sanders. Berkeley: University of California Press, 1984. Originally published as *L'Art: Entretiens réunis part Paul Gsell/Auguste Rodin*. Paris: Bernard Grasset, 1911.

Steinberg, Leo. "Rodin." In *Other Criteria: Confrontations with Twentieth-Century Art*, 322–403. New York: Oxford University Press, 1972.

Tancock, John. *The Sculptures of Auguste Rodin: The Collection of the Rodin Museum in Philadelphia*. Philadelphia: Philadelphia Museum of Art, 1976.

Thorson, Victoria. *Rodin Graphics: A Catalogue Raisonné of Drypoints and Books*. San Francisco: Fine Arts Museums of San Francisco, 1975.

Thanks to Our Generous Friends.

The B. Gerald Cantor Rodin Sculpture Garden was established with generous support from the following donors:

FOUNDER Mr. B. Gerald Cantor

BENEFACTOR Pepsico Foundation, Incorporated

PATRONS Anonymous Donor, The Estate of Elinor V. Cogswell, Mr. and Mrs. Irving Carlton Deal, Mrs. Robin Quist, Mrs. Paul L. Wattis

SPONSORS Mr. Michael James Collins, Mr. and Mrs. Thomas J. Davis, Jr., Albert and Patricia Elsen, Mr. and Mrs. Laszlo Fono, Mr. and Mrs. Robert M. Halperin, The Robert Klein Family, Mr. and Mrs. Patrick Maveety, Stanford Club of Palo Alto, Ed and Virginia Tomaso, Mr. Toby Wilcox, Mr. Charles J. Wilson

DONORS Mr. and Mrs. Ellis J. Alden, H. W. and M. M. Anderson Charitable Foundation, Mr. and Mrs. L. Burt Avery, Mr. Eaton W. Ballard, Mr. Mason Jay Blacher, Mrs. Elmira M. Bravos, in memory of Louis T. Bravos, Dr. Theodore A. Bravos in memory of Evelyn M. Bravos, Brooks Products, Inc., in memory of Dana Brooks Connolly, M.D. '71, Mr. and Mrs. C. S. Chapman, Jr., Mr. Edwin Henry Clock, Dr. Thomas F. Conroy, Mr. Ben C. Deane, Ruth and Jerome Debs, Mr. and Mrs. John Freidenrich, Professor and Mrs. James F. Gibbons, Mrs. Richard I. Gonzalez, Dr. Jean Haber Green, Mr. Gordon F. Hampton, Professor and Mrs. Paul R. Hanna, Mr. and Mrs. James Kresl, Mr. John August Kriewall, Mr. Albert Kurtzon, Mr. and Mrs. Hoyt B. Leisure, Mr. and Mrs. George Roy Liddle, Mr. and Mrs. William L. Lowe, Dr. and Mrs. Burton J. McMurtry, Mrs. James R. McNamara, Mrs. Jane B. Miller, Mr. and Mrs. Charles T. Munger, Napa Valley Stanford Club, in memory of Allan Green, M.D. '46 (1922–1984), Mr. and Mrs. Merrill E. Newman, Mr. and Mrs. C. Y. Offutt, Jr., Claire Perry, Mr. and Mrs. Thomas P. Pike, Jack and Marjorie Power, Mr. and Mrs. Robert M. Rees, Mr. and Mrs. Moey Segal, Mr. John Dickerson Smith, Mrs. Jane Henry Sousa, Mrs. Eugenie B. Taylor, Mr. Donovan Thayer, Transamerica Corporation (matching gift), Wells Fargo Foundation (matching gift)

CONTRIBUTORS Anonymous Donor, Mrs. Richard E. Abbott, Ms. Helen J. Ackerman, Mr. Thornton V. Allen, Jr., American Society for Surgery of the Hand, Ms. Barbara A. Ames, Mr. and Mrs. Richard T. Baker, Bank of America Foundation (matching gift), Mr. and Mrs. Melvin R. Bennington, Mr. and Mrs. James C. Benson, Mrs. Florence W. Berger, Mrs. Anne K. Berry, Mrs. Walter T. Bogart, Mr. and Mrs. Sheldon Breiner, Miss Pauline Brown, Mr. Gene J. Burton, Mr. John Cammidge, Mr. Robert A. Capwell, Mr. and Mrs. Richard C. Carey, Mr. Courtney Catron, Dr. and Mrs. Robert A. Chase, Michael Cohen, Augustus J. Conoscente, Miss Alice Coogan, Mr. and Mrs. Robert B. Crawford, Mrs. Ralph K.

Davies, Mrs. Robin Decius, Mr. Emerson Depuy, Dr. and Mrs. Kenneth V. Dole, Mr. and Mrs. Jon Eisenson, Dr. Theodore G. Eschenbach, Mrs. Virginia Escher, Mr. Bruce Fadem, Mrs. Betty E. Field, Mr. and Mrs. Charles D. Field, Harriet and Murray L. Finebaum, Mr. George Gaber, Mr. William C. Georges, Ms. Agnes H. Goss, Mrs. Arthur Graham, Mr. and Mrs. Gerald Grinstein, Marylin K. Gunderson, Mr. and Mrs. Herman Halperin, Dr. and Mrs. John W. Hanbery, Mrs. Louise Harris, Mr. and Mrs. John Hays, Mrs. Jane K. Hoffman, Mr. and Mrs. Ramiel M. Howitt, Ms. Helen M. Hunt, Mrs. Carolyn M. Hutchinson, Ms. Linda C. Jones, Mr. and Mrs. Richard B. Kilner, Dr. Esther M. Lederberg, Mr. and Mrs. F. Jack Liebau, Mr. and Mrs. Harry A. Louchheim, Mr. and Mrs. Raymond A. Marks, Dr. Jody Maxmin, Mrs. Jane Milne, Mr. and Mrs. Albert J. Moorman, Dr. and Mrs. Niles R. Moseley, The Museum Society of the M. H. deYoung Memorial Museum, Mr. and Mrs. Philip J. O'Donnell, Ms. Elizabeth Paschal, Mrs. Sandi O'Brien Patterson, Mrs. Fran Ragno, Mrs. Louise Reed, Mrs. Jinny Reinhardt, Dr. and Mrs. Paul Reinhardt, in honor of Bill and Mary Lou Corbus, Dr. and Mrs. Marvin D. Richards, Mr. and Mrs. Frank H. Roberts, Mr. Henry E. Robison, Mr. and Mrs. Leo Roselyn, Saga Corporation (matching gift), Mr. Ralph Schaffner, Mrs. Sherman R. Selix, Mrs. Andrew M. Spears, Mrs. Marilyn Spiegl, Stanford Bachelors, Stanford Club of Los Gatos/Saratoga, Stanford Club of Sacramento, Stanford Club of the South Bay, Stanford East Bay Metro Club, Stanford Nurse Alumnae, Stanford Women of the East Bay, Mr. and Mrs. Stewart H. Steere, Mr. David H. Steinmetz, Mr. and Mrs. John Olerich Steiny, Mr. John A. Sturgeon, Mrs. Lorraine Thackery, Ms. Marion J. Theobald, in memory of Ruth Saxe, Miss Diane Jane Thoreau, Lauren D. Upson, Ms. Charlotte H. Upton, Mrs. John A. Vibert, Mrs. Betsy Walker, Dr. William Michael Wara, Mrs. Elise Watkins, Mr. and Mrs. T. Joseph Willits

In conjunction with the opening of the Cantor Arts Center in 1999 several improvements were made to the B. Gerald Cantor Rodin Sculpture Garden. We thank the following donors for their support of these enhancements.

BENEFACTORS Melitta and Rex Vaughan

PATRONS Anonymous Donor, Mr. and Mrs. Robert P. Mann, Palo Alto University Rotary Club

SPONSORS Greater Bay Bancorp Foundation, Mr. and Mrs. Roger Mertz, Geri and Donovan Thayer

DONORS Harriet and Nathan Brenner Family, Melissa and Kenneth D. Brenner Family, Judy, Ronald, and Adam Brenner, Mrs. Jonathan B. Gifford, David and Helen MacKenzie, The W.O.O.D. Foundation

INDEX

Page numbers in italic refer to illustrations.

COPY EDITOR: KAREN JACOBSON, CULVER CITY, CALIFORNIA
PHOTO EDITOR: ALICJA T. EGBERT

Produced by Wilsted & Taylor Publishing Services

PRODUCTION MANAGEMENT: CHRISTINE TAYLOR
DESIGN AND COMPOSITION: JEFF CLARK
PRINTED IN HONG KONG THROUGH
QUINNESSENTIALS BOOKS AND PRINTING, INC.